The Supreme 15

The Supreme 15

*Cases and Study Materials for
AP Government and Politics Exam*

Gretchen Oltman
Johnna L. Graff
Cynthia Wood Maddux

ROWMAN & LITTLEFIELD
Lanham • Boulder • New York • London

Published by Rowman & Littlefield
An imprint of The Rowman & Littlefield Publishing Group, Inc.
4501 Forbes Boulevard, Suite 200, Lanham, Maryland 20706
www.rowman.com

6 Tinworth Street, London SE11 5AL

Copyright © 2019 by Gretchen Oltman, Johnna L. Graff, and Cynthia Wood Maddux

All rights reserved. No part of this book may be reproduced in any form or by any electronic or mechanical means, including information storage and retrieval systems, without written permission from the publisher, except by a reviewer who may quote passages in a review.

British Library Cataloguing in Publication Information Available

Library of Congress Cataloging-in-Publication Data

Names: Graff, Johnna L., 1974- author. | Maddux, Cynthia Wood, 1964- author. | Oltman, Gretchen A., author.
Title: The supreme 15 : cases and study materials for AP government and politics exam / Johnna Graff, Cynthia Wood Maddux, Gretchen Oltman.
Description: Lanham : Rowman & Littlefield 2019. | Includes bibliographical references and index. | Summary: "This book engages readers with the edited texts of the required 15 U.S. Supreme Court cases necessary to prepare for the AP Politics and Government exam. Guidance is provided to assist with vocabulary, complex legal analysis, reading questions, and extension possibilities to promote thinking about the application of the cases in new settings"—Provided by publisher.
Identifiers: LCCN 2019012953 (print) | LCCN 2019980814 (ebook) | ISBN 9781475849363 (cloth) | ISBN 9781475849370 (paperback) | ISBN 9781475849387 (ebook)
Subjects: LCSH: Constitutional law—United States—Examinations—Study guides. | Advanced placement programs (Education)—Examinations—Study guides. | United States—Politics and government—Examinations—Study guides. | Constitutional law—Study and teaching (Secondary)—United States. | LCGFT: Study guides. | Casebooks (Law)
Classification: LCC KF4208.5.L3 G73 2019 (print) | LCC KF4208.5.L3 (ebook) | DDC 342.73/0076—dc23
LC record available at https://lccn.loc.gov/2019012953
LC ebook record available at https://lccn.loc.gov/2019980814

To our students who have shown us the importance of and need for legal literacy.

Contents

Introduction: Reading U.S. Supreme Court Cases in the AP Classroom   ix

1. *Marbury v. Madison*   1
2. *McCulloch v. Maryland*   13
3. *Schenck v. United States*   29
4. *Brown v. Board of Education of Topeka*   35
5. *Baker v. Carr*   43
6. *Engel v. Vitale*   57
7. *Gideon v. Wainwright*   67
8. *Tinker v. Des Moines Independent Community School District*   75
9. *New York Times Co. v. United States*   83
10. *Wisconsin v. Yoder*   101
11. *Roe v. Wade*   109
12. *Shaw v. Reno*   125
13. *United States v. Lopez*   137
14. *Citizens United v. Federal Election Commission*   145
15. *McDonald v. Chicago*   165

Index   189

About the Authors   193

Introduction

Reading U.S. Supreme Court Cases in the AP Classroom

Beginning fall 2018, the College Board's Advanced Placement (AP) Program released a new course and exam description for the Advanced Placement Government and Politics course. This revision of course materials called for the restructuring of outcomes and provided some guidance on how students could more adequately prepare for the exam by identifying key primary documents. One of these new features includes a list of fifteen U.S. Supreme Court cases. Students learn to analyze these landmark cases by comparing information within the cases to new fact scenarios and other court decisions and applying them in new legal settings. In addition to studying these cases, students also investigate other texts and materials that build a foundational understanding of U.S. politics.

Students are clearly expected to do more than recite case holdings and regurgitate basic case facts. The College Board undoubtedly expects students to read and study U.S. Supreme Court case law for its analytical properties and the development of arguments. The College Board presents this impassioned argument to teachers of AP Government and Politics courses stating:

> AP U.S. Government and Politics offers students the opportunity to see how individuals and their ideas can shape the world in which they live; it invites them to explore central questions of liberty and justice in practice. The Supreme Court opinions explored in this course are not museum pieces but deeply felt expressions. They all represent real choices and decisions with enormous consequences. We aim for students to read them and discuss them with openness and insight. (College Board 2018, 7)

This is a compelling insight and yet quite challenging to think about practically. That is, in one class period, with one teacher, with one set of materials, students will become critical thinkers about political and legal issues from years ago to those emerging today. What is expected of students is to be more than consumers of current events and national news—they should be informed analysts of argument and reasoning. Disciplinary reading, utilizing a set of reading skills required to comprehend and understand a specific field of content—like history or political science—requires the guidance of a teacher. Providing students a list of cases to study lacks what the College Board is asking students to do: analyze documents and debates, develop a "Command of the Constitution," and study with "principled attention" (7).

READING U.S. SUPREME COURT CASES WITHIN AN AP GOPO COURSE

It is important to realize that although there is a list of fifteen U.S. Supreme Court cases to prepare for the AP Government and Politics exam, those fifteen cases do not exist in solitude nor are the cases exclusive to what students need to know for the course or the exam. The College Board lists four disciplinary practices students should utilize in regard to the study of U.S. Supreme Court cases. Student are challenged to apply U.S. Supreme Court cases by:

- describing the facts, reasoning, decision, and majority opinion of required Supreme Court cases;
- explaining how a required U.S. Supreme Court case relates to a foundational document or to other primary or secondary sources;
- comparing the reasoning, decision, and majority opinion of a required U.S. Supreme Court case to a non-required U.S. Supreme Court case; and
- explaining how required Supreme Court cases apply to scenarios in context. (College Board 2018, 10).

Students will need to move beyond reciting a Court holding to understanding *how* and *why* the Court sets forth its decisions. The College Board notes the depth students must examine Court cases stating, "This includes how holdings are decided and that justices who are in the minority often write dissents that express their opinions on the case and the Constitutional questions. While students will not need to know any dissenting (or concurring) opinions from the required cases, it is important for students to understand the role of dissenting opinions, especially as they relate to future cases on similar issues" (44). Thus, while students do need to know the how and why of a decision, they will also be challenged to know the *counterarguments* or rationale for differing opinions. Needless to say, lawyers spend years perfecting this craft, so high-school students will need teacher guidance and assistance to do so effectively.

FEATURES OF THIS BOOK

Teaching students how to read U.S. Supreme Court case law (or any case law) can be accomplished by teaching students how to identify the same main parts of a case: the facts, the issue, the holding, and the reason behind the decision. These are the same basic methods law students use to learn how to read cases. However, high-school students are not lawyers, so we also recommend assisting students with difficult vocabulary, providing reading guidance to prompt critical thinking and questioning during the study of the case, and encouraging structured reading help to enable readers to grow comfortable with the tone, style, and method of reading a case.

It is important to note that this book was written in light of the many resources available online to both teachers and students. In our work, we recognize the inherent challenges of teaching fifteen U.S. Supreme Court cases and multiple primary documents amid the daily life of classroom activities. However, in our work with teachers, we noticed a troubling trend: providing students short outlines or summaries of cases rather than having students muddle through the actual cases.

While it is entirely possible for students to learn case names and holdings through rote memorization, the higher-level critical-thinking skills intended to be employed through the AP framework is missed. Students are not learning how to tangle with language, wrestle with differing justices' opinions, or deduce the actual reason a case may have ended the way it did. When asked to apply the Court's rationale to a new scenario or to compare one case to another, a student is lost with no thorough background information on which to rely. So, while we appreciate the tone and effort utilized in trying to teach this material to students, we must also keep in mind the overall goal of the learning, which is to apply those critical-thinking skills in multiple ways.

This book was written with the expectation that students *should* be wading within the pages of U.S. Supreme Court decisions. This book also keeps a scholarly mindset at the forefront as it examines the fifteen cases identified by the AP College Board. Clearly, the language, word choices, and structures used by the U.S. Supreme Court justices are eloquent and thought provoking. The decisions are widely available for free through government websites and other Internet sources. Many are quite long, will require multiple readings, and present demanding vocabulary; however, this is exactly what the College Board is challenging students to do through active reading. Thus, we have carefully read, reviewed, and edited each of the fifteen selected cases to assist the adolescent reader and have included the following teaching and reading features:

- original language was left intact, but distractors were removed (those distractors include citations to additional cases, ancillary discussions by justices, and some procedural information);
- a short background to orient the reader to the historical framework for each case;
- a clear delineation of the parties within each case (basically, who is suing who?);
- identification of the legal question examined within the case as well as applicable constitutional law applied;
- challenging vocabulary words were identified within each case and offered with definitions for use in context;
- reading questions were strategically placed within each case to guide a reader through the analysis and reasoning of the Court; and
- opportunities at the end of each chapter provide extension questions and activities for the reader, including hypotheticals to apply the case reasoning and discussion of another court case to allow the reader to compare and contrast facts between cases.

If the end goal is for students to become informed citizens and be able to understand new cases as they emerge from the court, it is imperative that students begin to see the commonalities of cases and the ways in which the everyday reader can access and apply new holdings in new generations. The practice through these fifteen cases does just that: it engages the reader, acknowledges challenging content, and provides analytical exercises to extend learning.

REFERENCE

The College Board (2018). AP U.S. Government and Politics: Course and Exam Description. Retrieved from http://apcentral.collegeboard.org.

Chapter One

Marbury v. Madison

Article III, Section 2 of the U.S. Constitution reads, "In all Cases affecting Ambassadors, other public Ministers and Consuls, and those in which a State shall be Party, the supreme Court shall have original Jurisdiction. In all the other Cases before mentioned, the supreme Court shall have appellate Jurisdiction, both as to Law and Fact, with such Exceptions, and under such Regulations as the Congress shall make."

Before Thomas Jefferson was inaugurated in 1801, the lame-duck Congress created a number of new judgeships, and outgoing President John Adams filled the openings with Federalist appointees to preserve his party's judicial control. William Marbury, a Federalist, did not receive his commission before Jefferson was sworn in, and President Jefferson instructed his secretary of state, James Madison, to withhold it. Marbury went to the Supreme Court seeking a writ of mandamus to get his judgeship.

Chief Justice John Marshall recognized that beyond issuing a writ of mandamus there were larger issues at hand: if the Court had issued the writ, Jefferson could simply ignore it because the Court could not enforce it, but if the Court just went along with Jefferson, the Court would look as if it was simply acquiescing to Jefferson's wishes. Justice Marshall wanted to make it clear what he believed was the true power of the Supreme Court: to be the ultimate arbiter of constitutional review.

Marshall's decision in *Marbury v. Madison* has been hailed as the most important decision in American constitutional law.

Legal Issue

What is the role of the U.S. Supreme Court?

Vocabulary

Mandamus: a judicial writ issued by a superior court commanding the performance of a specified official act or duty.
Civil liberty: freedom from arbitrary governmental interference.
Jurisdiction: the power, right, or authority to interpret and apply the law.

Parties in the Case

Petitioner: William Marbury, judicial appointee under President John Adams
Respondent: James Madison, secretary of state for President Thomas Jefferson
   Edited version of case in the original language with distractors removed.

MARBURY V. MADISON, 5 U.S. 137 (1803)

Mr. Chief Justice MARSHALL delivered the opinion of the Court.

At the last term, on the affidavits then read and filed with the clerk, a rule was granted in this case requiring the secretary of state to show cause why a mandamus should not issue directing him to deliver to William Marbury his commission as a justice of the peace for the county of Washington, in the District of Columbia.

No cause has been shown, and the present motion is for a mandamus. The peculiar delicacy of this case, the novelty of some of its circumstances, and the real difficulty attending the points which occur in it require a complete exposition of the principles on which the opinion to be given by the Court is founded.

In the order in which the Court has viewed this subject, the following questions have been considered and decided.

1. Has the applicant a right to the commission he demands?

His right originates in an act of Congress passed in February, 1801, concerning the District of Columbia.

It appears from the affidavits that, in compliance with this law, a commission for William Marbury as a justice of peace for the County of Washington was signed by John Adams, then president of the United States, after which the seal of the United States was affixed to it, but the commission has never reached the person for whom it was made out.

- *Who prevented Marbury from receiving his commission? Why do you think that person failed to deliver it to him?*

In order to determine whether he is entitled to this commission, it becomes necessary to inquire whether he has been appointed to the office. For if he has been appointed, the law continues him in office for five years, and he is entitled to the possession of those evidences of office, which, being completed, became his property.

The second section of the second article of the Constitution declares,

> The president shall nominate, and, by and with the advice and consent of the Senate, shall appoint ambassadors, other public ministers and consuls, and all other officers of the United States, whose appointments are not otherwise provided for.

The third section declares, that "He shall commission all the officers of the United States."

An act of Congress directs the secretary of state to keep the seal of the United States,

> to make out and record, and affix the said seal to all civil commissions to officers of the United States to be appointed by the president, by and with the consent of the Senate, or by the president alone; provided that the said seal shall not be affixed to any commission before the same shall have been signed by the president of the United States.

These are the clauses of the Constitution and laws of the United States which affect this part of the case. They seem to contemplate three distinct operations:

1. The nomination. This is the sole act of the president, and is completely voluntary.
2. The appointment. This is also the act of the president, and is also a voluntary act, though it can only be performed by and with the advice and consent of the Senate.
3. The commission. To grant a commission to a person appointed might perhaps be deemed a duty enjoined by the Constitution. "He shall," says that instrument, "commission all the officers of the United States."

It is therefore decidedly the opinion of the Court that, when a commission has been signed by the president, the appointment is made, and that the commission is complete when the seal of the United States has been affixed to it by the Secretary of State.

Where an officer is removable at the will of the Executive, the circumstance which completes his appointment is of no concern, because the act is at any time revocable, and the commission may be arrested if still in the office. But when the officer is not removable at the will of the Executive, the appointment is not revocable, and cannot be annulled. It has conferred legal rights which cannot be resumed.

The discretion of the Executive is to be exercised until the appointment has been made. But having once made the appointment, his power over the office is terminated in all cases, where by law the officer is not removable by him. The right to the office is then in the person appointed, and he has the absolute, unconditional power of accepting or rejecting it.

Mr. Marbury, then, since his commission was signed by the president and sealed by the secretary of state, was appointed, and as the law creating the office gave the officer a right to hold for five years independent of the Executive, the appointment was not revocable, but vested in the officer legal rights which are protected by the laws of his country.

- *Justice Marshall discusses two distinct presidential appointments. In one, the president has the right to terminate the position—"removable at will"—but the other is when the appointment is not removable by the president. Which do you think Marbury says he has?*

To withhold the commission, therefore, is an act deemed by the Court not warranted by law, but violative of a vested legal right.

This brings us to the second inquiry, which is:

2. If he has a right, and that right has been violated, do the laws of his country afford him a remedy?

The very essence of civil liberty certainly consists in the right of every individual to claim the protection of the laws whenever he receives an injury. One of the first duties of government is to afford that protection. In Great Britain, the king himself is sued in the respectful form of a petition, and he never fails to comply with the judgment of his court.

- *Why do you think Justice Marshall is pointing out that even the king in Great Britain can be sued? Who is Marshall implying is subject to the Court in this case?*

The government of the United States has been emphatically termed a government of laws, and not of men. It will certainly cease to deserve this high appellation if the laws furnish no remedy for the violation of a vested legal right.

It behooves us, then, to inquire whether there be in its composition any ingredient which shall exempt from legal investigation or exclude the injured party from legal redress. In pursuing this inquiry, the first question which presents itself is whether this can be arranged with that class of cases which come under the description of *damnum absque injuria*—a loss without an injury.

This description of cases never has been considered, and, it is believed, never can be considered, as comprehending offices of trust, of honour or of profit. The office of justice of peace in the District of Columbia is such an office; it is therefore worthy of the attention and guardianship of the laws. It has received that attention and guardianship. It has been created by special act of Congress, and has been secured, so far as the laws can give security to the person appointed to fill it, for five years. It is not then on account of the worthlessness of the thing pursued that the injured party can be alleged to be without remedy.

- *Justice Marshall says that in order to have a legal remedy the object in question must have some value. What does Marshall says is the value of being a justice of the peace?*

Is it in the nature of the transaction? Is the act of delivering or withholding a commission to be considered as a mere political act belonging to the Executive department alone, for the performance of which entire confidence is placed by our Constitution in the Supreme Executive, and for any misconduct respecting which the injured individual has no remedy?

- *Again, who is Justice Marshall accusing at for causing this issue to arise?*

That there may be such cases is not to be questioned, but that every act of duty to be performed in any of the great departments of government constitutes such a case is not to be admitted.

By the Constitution of the United States, the president is invested with certain important political powers, in the exercise of which he is to use his own discretion, and is accountable only to his country in his political character and to his own conscience. To aid him in the performance of these duties, he is authorized to appoint certain officers, who act by his authority and in conformity with his orders.

In such cases, their acts are his acts; and whatever opinion may be entertained of the manner in which executive discretion may be used, still there exists, and can exist, no power to control that discretion. The subjects are political. They respect the nation, not individual rights, and, being entrusted to the Executive, the decision of the Executive is conclusive. The application of this remark will be perceived by adverting to the act of Congress for establishing the Department of Foreign Affairs. This officer, as his duties were prescribed by that act, is to conform precisely to the will of the president. He is the mere organ by whom that will is communicated. The acts of such an officer, as an officer, can never be examinable by the Courts.

But when the Legislature proceeds to impose on that officer other duties; when he is directed peremptorily to perform certain acts; when the rights of individuals are dependent on the performance of those acts; he is so far the officer of the law, is amenable to the laws for his conduct, and cannot at his discretion, sport away the vested rights of others.

- *What is the difference, according to the opinion of the Court, whether "officers" of the president can act solely at the direction of the president? When are these "officers" required to act differently?*

The conclusion from this reasoning is that, where the heads of departments are the political or confidential agents of the Executive, merely to execute the will of the president, or rather to act in cases in which the Executive possesses a constitutional or legal discretion, nothing can be more perfectly clear than that their acts are only politically examinable. But where a specific duty is assigned by law, and individual rights depend upon the performance of that duty, it seems equally clear that the individual who considers himself injured has a right to resort to the laws of his country for a remedy.

The power of nominating to the Senate, and the power of appointing the person nominated, are political powers, to be exercised by the president according to his own discretion. When he has made an appointment, he has exercised his whole power, and his discretion has been completely applied to the case. If, by law, the officer be removable at the will of the president, then a new appointment may be immediately made, and the rights of the officer are terminated. But as a fact which has existed cannot be made never to have existed, the appointment cannot be annihilated, and consequently, if the officer is by law not removable at the will of the president, the rights he has acquired are protected by the law, and are not resumable by the president. They cannot be extinguished by Executive authority, and he has the privilege of asserting them in like manner as if they had been derived from any other source.

It is then the opinion of the Court:

1. That, by signing the commission of Mr. Marbury, the president of the United States appointed him a justice of peace for the County of Washington in the District of Columbia, and that the seal of the United States, affixed thereto by the secretary of state, is conclusive testimony of the verity of the signature, and of the completion of the appointment, and that the appointment conferred on him a legal right to the office for the space of five years.

2. That, having this legal title to the office, he has a consequent right to the commission, a refusal to deliver which is a plain violation of that right, for which the laws of his country afford him a remedy.

It remains to be inquired whether,

3. He is entitled to the remedy for which he applies. This depends on:

　　1. The nature of the writ applied for, and

2. The power of this court.

It is true that the mandamus now moved for is not for the performance of an act expressly enjoined by statute.

It is to deliver a commission, on which subjects the acts of Congress are silent. This difference is not considered as affecting the case. It has already been stated that the applicant has, to that commission, a vested legal right of which the Executive cannot deprive him. He has been appointed to an office from which he is not removable at the will of the Executive, and, being so appointed, he has a right to the commission which the secretary has received from the president for his use. The act of Congress does not, indeed, order the secretary of state to send it to him, but it is placed in his hands for the person entitled to it, and cannot be more lawfully withheld by him than by another person.

This, then, is a plain case of a mandamus, either to deliver the commission or a copy of it from the record, and it only remains to be inquired:

Whether it can issue from this Court.

The act to establish the judicial courts of the United States authorizes the Supreme Court "to issue writs of mandamus, in cases warranted by the principles and usages of law, to any courts appointed, or persons holding office, under the authority of the United States."

The secretary of state, being a person, holding an office under the authority of the United States, is precisely within the letter of the description, and if this Court is not authorized to issue a writ of mandamus to such an officer, it must be because the law is unconstitutional, and therefore absolutely incapable of conferring the authority and assigning the duties which its words purport to confer and assign.

- *To whom is the Court saying it has the power to issue a writ of mandamus?*

The Constitution vests the whole judicial power of the United States in one Supreme Court, and such inferior courts as Congress shall, from time to time, ordain and establish. This power is expressly extended to all cases arising under the laws of the United States; and consequently, in some form, may be exercised over the present case, because the right claimed is given by a law of the United States.

In the distribution of this power, it is declared that "The Supreme Court shall have original jurisdiction in all cases affecting ambassadors, other public ministers and consuls, and those in which a state shall be a party. In all other cases, the Supreme Court shall have appellate jurisdiction."

It has been insisted at the bar, that, as the original grant of jurisdiction to the Supreme and inferior courts is general, and the clause assigning original jurisdiction to the Supreme Court contains no negative or restrictive words, the power remains to the Legislature to assign original jurisdiction to that Court in other cases than those specified in the article which has been recited, provided those cases belong to the judicial power of the United States.

If it had been intended to leave it in the discretion of the Legislature to apportion the judicial power between the Supreme and inferior courts according to the will of that body, it would certainly have been useless to have proceeded further than to have defined the judicial power and the tribunals in which it should be vested. The subsequent part of the section is mere surplusage—is entirely without meaning—if such is to be the construction. If Congress remains at liberty to give this court appellate jurisdiction where the Constitution has declared their jurisdiction shall be original, and original jurisdiction where the Constitution has declared it shall be appellate, the distribution of jurisdiction made in the Constitution, is form without substance.

- *What argument does the Court use to say that it has power to decide legal issues and it doesn't need to wait for Congress to give it additional authority?*

Affirmative words are often, in their operation, negative of other objects than those affirmed, and, in this case, a negative or exclusive sense must be given to them or they have no operation at all.

It cannot be presumed that any clause in the Constitution is intended to be without effect, and therefore such construction is inadmissible unless the words require it.

To enable this court then to issue a mandamus, it must be shown to be an exercise of appellate jurisdiction, or to be necessary to enable them to exercise appellate jurisdiction.

It has been stated at the bar that the appellate jurisdiction may be exercised in a variety of forms, and that, if it be the will of the Legislature that a mandamus should be used for that purpose, that will must be obeyed. This is true; yet the jurisdiction must be appellate, not original.

It is the essential criterion of appellate jurisdiction that it revises and corrects the proceedings in a cause already instituted, and does not create that case. Although, therefore, a mandamus may be directed to courts, yet to issue such a writ to an officer for the delivery of a paper is, in effect, the same as to sustain an original action for that paper, and therefore seems not to belong to appellate, but to original jurisdiction. Neither is it necessary in such a case as this to enable the Court to exercise its appellate jurisdiction.

The authority, therefore, given to the Supreme Court by the act establishing the judicial courts of the United States to issue writs of mandamus to public officers appears not to be warranted by the Constitution, and it becomes necessary to inquire whether a jurisdiction so conferred can be exercised.

- *The Court says it doesn't have the authority to issue Marbury's writ of mandamus. What reason does it give?*

The question whether an act repugnant to the Constitution can become the law of the land is a question deeply interesting to the United States, but, happily, not of an intricacy proportioned to its interest. It seems only necessary to recognise certain principles, supposed to have been long and well established, to decide it.

That the people have an original right to establish for their future government such principles as, in their opinion, shall most conduce to their own happiness is the basis on which the whole American fabric has been erected. The exercise of this original right is a very great exertion; nor can it nor ought it to be frequently repeated. The principles, therefore, so established are deemed fundamental. And as the authority from which they proceed, is supreme, and can seldom act, they are designed to be permanent.

This original and supreme will organizes the government and assigns to different departments their respective powers. It may either stop here or establish certain limits not to be transcended by those departments.

The Government of the United States is of the latter description. The powers of the Legislature are defined and limited; and that those limits may not be mistaken or forgotten, the Constitution is written. To what purpose are powers limited, and to what purpose is that limitation committed to writing, if these limits may at any time be passed by those intended to be restrained? The distinction between a government with limited and unlimited powers is abolished if those limits do not confine the persons on whom they are imposed, and if acts prohibited and acts allowed are of equal obligation. It is a proposition too plain to be contested that the Constitution controls any legislative act repugnant to it, or that the Legislature may alter the Constitution by an ordinary act.

Between these alternatives there is no middle ground. The Constitution is either a superior, paramount law, unchangeable by ordinary means, or it is on a level with ordinary legislative acts, and, like other acts, is alterable when the legislature shall please to alter it.

This theory is essentially attached to a written Constitution, and is consequently to be considered by this Court as one of the fundamental principles of our society. It is not, therefore, to be lost sight of in the further consideration of this subject.

If an act of the Legislature repugnant to the Constitution is void, does it, notwithstanding its invalidity, bind the Courts and oblige them to give it effect? Or, in other words, though it be not law, does it constitute a rule as operative as if it was a law? This would be to overthrow in fact what was established in theory, and would seem, at first view, an absurdity too gross to be insisted on. It shall, however, receive a more attentive consideration.

It is emphatically the province and duty of the Judicial Department to say what the law is. Those who apply the rule to particular cases must, of necessity, expound and interpret that rule. If two laws conflict with each other, the Courts must decide on the operation of each.

- *What important power has the Court just indicated that it has?*

So, if a law be in opposition to the Constitution, if both the law and the Constitution apply to a particular case, so that the Court must either decide that case conformably to the law, disregarding the Constitution, or conformably to the Constitution, disregarding the law, the Court must determine which of these conflicting rules governs the case. This is of the very essence of judicial duty.

If, then, the Courts are to regard the Constitution, and the Constitution is superior to any ordinary act of the Legislature, the Constitution, and not such ordinary act, must govern the case to which they both apply.

This doctrine would subvert the very foundation of all written Constitutions. It would declare that an act which, according to the principles and theory of our government, is entirely void, is yet, in practice, completely obligatory. It would declare that, if the Legislature shall do what is expressly forbidden, such act, notwithstanding the express prohibition, is in reality effectual. It would be giving to the Legislature a practical and real omnipotence with the same breath which professes to restrict their powers within narrow limits. It is prescribing limits, and declaring that those limits may be passed at pleasure.

That it thus reduces to nothing what we have deemed the greatest improvement on political institutions—a written Constitution, would of itself be sufficient, in America where written Constitutions have been viewed with so much reverence, for rejecting the construction. But the peculiar expressions of the Constitution of the United States furnish additional arguments in favour of its rejection.

The judicial power of the United States is extended to all cases arising under the Constitution.

- *After the Court decides it cannot issue Marbury's writ of mandamus, how has the Court gone on to declare what the role of the Supreme Court is?*

Could it be the intention of those who gave this power to say that, in using it, the Constitution should not be looked into? That a case arising under the

Constitution should be decided without examining the instrument under which it arises?

This is too extravagant to be maintained.

[I]t is apparent that the framers of the Constitution contemplated that instrument as a rule for the government of courts, as well as of the Legislature.

Why otherwise does it direct the judges to take an oath to support it? This oath certainly applies in an especial manner to their conduct in their official character. How immoral to impose it on them if they were to be used as the instruments, and the knowing instruments, for violating what they swear to support!

The oath of office, too, imposed by the Legislature, is completely demonstrative of the legislative opinion on this subject. It is in these words:

> I do solemnly swear that I will administer justice without respect to persons, and do equal right to the poor and to the rich; and that I will faithfully and impartially discharge all the duties incumbent on me as according to the best of my abilities and understanding, agreeably to the Constitution and laws of the United States.

Why does a judge swear to discharge his duties agreeably to the Constitution of the United States if that Constitution forms no rule for his government? if it is closed upon him and cannot be inspected by him?

- *What evidence does the Court use to support the idea that the framers intended for the Supreme Court to decide constitutional issues?*

Thus, the particular phraseology of the Constitution of the United States confirms and strengthens the principle, supposed to be essential to all written Constitutions, that a law repugnant to the Constitution is void, and that courts, as well as other departments, are bound by that instrument.

The rule must be discharged.

Connecting, Arguing, and Analyzing the Case

1. After reading *Marbury v. Madison*, describe "judicial" review in characters no longer than a Tweet (140 characters).
2. The writers of the Constitution were worried that the government would have too much power. How does the ruling in *Marbury v. Madison* enhance the system of checks and balances as envisioned by the founders of the U.S. government?
3. The decision in *Marbury v. Madison* has been criticized due to the fact that Supreme Court justices are not elected officials and do not have to answer to an electorate as they make their decisions. Construct an

argument where you propose that *Marbury v. Madison* be overturned with at least three different reasons.
4. How was Justice Marshall's decision supported by James Hamilton in his essay *Federalist No. 51*? By Alexander Hamilton in his essay *Federalist No. 78*?
5. In *Furman v. Georgia*, 408 U.S. 238 (1972), the death penalty in the United States was temporarily stopped by the U.S. Supreme Court. The Court ruled state death penalty statutes were not applied consistently or fairly enough to pass muster under the Eighth Amendment. What other cases can you find where the judicial review by the Supreme Court has affected legal changes across the entire nation?
6. In *United States v. Nixon*, 418 U.S. 683 (1974), the Supreme Court extended its judicial review to the actions of the president. Examine this case and then write a memorandum where you argue either for or against limiting judicial review to the executive branch of the government.

Chapter Two

McCulloch v. Maryland

Article I, Section 8 of the U.S. Constitution states, "The Congress shall have Power . . . To make all Laws which shall be necessary and proper for carrying into Execution the foregoing Powers, and all other Powers vested by this Constitution in the Government of the United States, or in any Department or Officer thereof." The "necessary and proper" clause, also called the "elastic clause," gives Congress the ability to make laws not enumerated by the Constitution. This clause provoked much controversy at Continental Congress, where anti-Federalists were worried that its inclusion would give the federal government unlimited power. However, Federalists Alexander Hamilton and James Madison argued for its inclusion, saying that without it, the Constitution would be a "dead letter."

The clause was used to justify the creation of the First National Bank of the United States, but it did not come under Supreme Court scrutiny until the State of Maryland sought to tax out-of-state banks, and at the time, the Second Bank of the United States was the only one in Maryland. James William McCulloch, the head of the Baltimore Branch of the Second Bank of the United States, refused to pay the tax. The decision in this case was seminal in determining the scope of federal legislative power and the relationship and authority states could have over federally created entities.

Legal Issue

Can the federal government create a bank, and if so, can individual states tax such a bank?

Vocabulary

Necessary: absolutely needed; required

Nugatory: of little or no consequence
Prolixity: unduly prolonged or drawn out; too long
Exigencies: that which is required in a particular situation
Axiom: an established rule or principle or a self-evident truth

Parties in this Case

Petitioner: James William McCulloch
Respondent: The State of Maryland
  Edited version of case in the original language with distractors removed.

MCCULLOCH V. MARYLAND, 17 U.S. 316 (1819)

MARSHALL, Chief Justice, delivered the opinion of the Court.

In the case now to be determined, the defendant, a sovereign state, denies the obligation of a law enacted by the legislature of the Union, and the plaintiff, on his part, contests the validity of an act which has been passed by the legislature of that state. The Constitution of our country, in its most interesting and vital parts, is to be considered, the conflicting powers of the government of the Union and of its members, as marked in that Constitution, are to be discussed, and an opinion given which may essentially influence the great operations of the government. No tribunal can approach such a question without a deep sense of its importance, and of the awful responsibility involved in its decision. But it must be decided peacefully, or remain a source of hostile legislation, perhaps, of hostility of a still more serious nature; and if it is to be so decided, by this tribunal alone can the decision be made. On the Supreme Court of the United States has the Constitution of our country devolved this important duty.

The first question made in the cause is—has Congress power to incorporate a bank?

The power now contested was exercised by the first Congress elected under the present Constitution.

The bill for incorporating the Bank of the United States did not steal upon an unsuspecting legislature and pass unobserved. Its principle was completely understood, and was opposed with equal zeal and ability. After being resisted first in the fair and open field of debate, and afterward in the executive cabinet, with as much persevering talent as any measure has ever experienced, and being supported by arguments which convinced minds as pure and as intelligent as this country can boast, it became a law. The original act was permitted to expire, but a short experience of the embarrassments to which the refusal to revive it exposed the government convinced those who were most prejudiced against the measure of its necessity, and induced the passage of the present law. It would require no ordinary share of intrepidity to assert that a measure adopted under these circumstances was a bold and plain usurpation to which the Constitution gave no countenance. These observations belong to the cause; but they are not made under the impression that, were the question entirely new, the law would be found irreconcilable with the Constitution.

- *What is the Court reminding the people of Maryland about in the preceding paragraph? Was the idea of a national bank just sprung on the people of the United States out of nowhere?*

In discussing this question, the counsel for the State of Maryland have deemed it of some importance, in the construction of the Constitution, to consider that instrument not as emanating from the people, but as the act of sovereign and independent states. The powers of the general government, it has been said, are delegated by the States, who alone are truly sovereign, and must be exercised in subordination to the states, who alone possess supreme dominion.

- *Why is it important that Justice Marshall bring up the fact that Maryland had a voice in the Constitution?*

It would be difficult to sustain this proposition. The convention which framed the Constitution was indeed elected by the state legislatures. But the instrument, when it came from their hands, was a mere proposal, without obligation or pretensions to it. It was reported to the then existing Congress of the United States with a request that it might "be submitted to a convention of delegates, chosen in each state by the people thereof, under the recommendation of its legislature, for their assent and ratification."

This mode of proceeding was adopted, and by the convention, by Congress, and by the state legislatures, the instrument was submitted to the people. They acted upon it in the only manner in which they can act safely, effectively and wisely, on such a subject—by assembling in convention. It is true, they assembled in their several states—and where else should they have assembled? No political dreamer was ever wild enough to think of breaking down the lines which separate the states, and of compounding the American people into one common mass. Of consequence, when they act, they act in their states. But the measures they adopt do not, on that account, cease to be the measures of the people themselves, or become the measures of the state governments.

From these conventions the Constitution derives its whole authority. The government proceeds directly from the people; is "ordained and established" in the name of the people, and is declared to be ordained, "in order to form a more perfect union, establish justice, insure domestic tranquillity, and secure the blessings of liberty to themselves and to their posterity."

The assent of the states in their sovereign capacity is implied in calling a convention, and thus submitting that instrument to the people. But the people were at perfect liberty to accept or reject it, and their act was final. It required not the affirmance, and could not be negatived, by the state governments. The Constitution, when thus adopted, was of complete obligation, and bound the state sovereignties.

It has been said that the people had already surrendered all their powers to the state sovereignties, and had nothing more to give. But surely the question whether they may resume and modify the powers granted to government does not remain to be settled in this country. Much more might the legitimacy of the general government be doubted had it been created by the states. The powers delegated to the State sovereignties were to be exercised by themselves, not by a distinct and independent sovereignty created by themselves.

To the formation of a league such as was the confederation, the state sovereignties were certainly competent. But when, "in order to form a more perfect union," it was deemed necessary to change this alliance into an effective government, possessing great and sovereign powers and acting directly on the people, the necessity of referring it to the people, and of deriving its powers directly from them, was felt and acknowledged by all. The government of the Union then (whatever may be the influence of this fact on the case) is, emphatically and truly, a government of the people. In form and in substance, it emanates from them. Its powers are granted by them, and are to be exercised directly on them, and for their benefit.

- *In the previous three paragraphs, why do you think Justice Marshall harkens back to the Preamble of the Constitution?*

This government is acknowledged by all to be one of enumerated powers. The principle that it can exercise only the powers granted to it would seem too apparent to have required to be enforced by all those arguments which its enlightened friends, while it was depending before the people, found it necessary to urge; that principle is now universally admitted. But the question respecting the extent of the powers actually granted is perpetually arising, and will probably continue to arise so long as our system shall exist. In discussing these questions, the conflicting powers of the general and state governments must be brought into view, and the supremacy of their respective laws, when they are in opposition, must be settled.

If any one proposition could command the universal assent of mankind, we might expect it would be this—that the government of the Union, though limited in its powers, is supreme within its sphere of action. This would seem to result necessarily from its nature. It is the government of all; its powers are delegated by all; it represents all, and acts for all. Though any one state may be willing to control its operations, no state is willing to allow others to control them.

- *What is Marshall saying about the powers of the federal government in relation to the powers of the individual states?*

The nation, on those subjects on which it can act, must necessarily bind its component parts. But this question is not left to mere reason; the people have, in express terms, decided it by saying, "this Constitution, and the laws of the United States, which shall be made in pursuance thereof," "shall be the supreme law of the land," and by requiring that the members of the state legislatures and the officers of the executive and judicial departments of the states shall take the oath of fidelity to it. The government of the United States, then, though limited in its powers, is supreme, and its laws, when made in pursuance of the Constitution, form the supreme law of the land, "anything in the Constitution or laws of any State to the contrary notwithstanding."

- *Why is this discussion of both limited power and supremacy important?*

Among the enumerated powers, we do not find that of establishing a bank or creating a corporation. But there is no phrase in the instrument which, like the Articles of Confederation, excludes incidental or implied powers and which requires that everything granted shall be expressly and minutely described. Even the 10th Amendment, which was framed for the purpose of quieting the excessive jealousies which had been excited, omits the word "expressly," and declares only that the powers "not delegated to the United States, nor prohibited to the States, are reserved to the States or to the people," thus leaving the question whether the particular power which may become the subject of contest has been delegated to the one Government, or prohibited to the other, to depend on a fair construction of the whole instrument. The men who drew and adopted this amendment had experienced the embarrassments resulting from the insertion of this word in the Articles of Confederation, and probably omitted it to avoid those embarrassments.

A Constitution, to contain an accurate detail of all the subdivisions of which its great powers will admit, and of all the means by which they may be carried into execution, would partake of the prolixity of a legal code, and could scarcely be embraced by the human mind. It would probably never be understood by the public. Its nature, therefore, requires that only its great outlines should be marked, its important objects designated, and the minor ingredients which compose those objects be deduced from the nature of the objects themselves.

- *Why is Marshall saying the Constitution was kept simple?*

That this idea was entertained by the framers of the American Constitution is not only to be inferred from the nature of the instrument, but from the language. Why else were some of the limitations found in the 9th section of the 1st article introduced? It is also in some degree warranted by their having omitted to use any restrictive term which might prevent its receiving a fair and just interpretation. In considering this question, then, we must never forget that it is a Constitution we are expounding.

Although, among the enumerated powers of government, we do not find the word "bank" or "incorporation," we find the great powers, to lay and collect taxes; to borrow money; to regulate commerce; to declare and conduct a war; and to raise and support armies and navies. The sword and the purse, all the external relations, and no inconsiderable portion of the industry of the nation are intrusted to its government. It can never be pretended that these vast powers draw after them others of inferior importance merely because they are inferior. Such an idea can never be advanced. But it may with great reason be contended that a government intrusted with such ample powers, on the due execution of which the happiness and prosperity of the nation so vitally depends, must also be intrusted with ample means for their execution. The power being given, it is the interest of the nation to facilitate its execution. It can never be their interest, and cannot be presumed to have been their intention, to clog and embarrass its execution by withholding the most appropriate means.

- *Marshall discusses the enumerated powers, but what else must necessarily flow from those enumerated powers so they can be successful?*

Throughout this vast republic, from the St. Croix to the Gulf of Mexico, from the Atlantic to the Pacific, revenue is to be collected and expended, armies are to be marched and supported. The exigencies of the nation may require that the treasure raised in the north should be transported to the south that raised in the east, conveyed to the west, or that this order should be reversed. Is that construction of the Constitution to be preferred which would render these operations difficult, hazardous and expensive? Can we adopt that construction (unless the words imperiously require it) which would impute to the framers of that instrument, when granting these powers for the public good, the intention of impeding their exercise, by withholding a choice of means? If, indeed, such be the mandate of the Constitution, we have only to obey; but that instrument does not profess to enumerate the means by which the powers it confers may be executed; nor does it prohibit the creation of a corporation, if the existence of such a being be essential, to the beneficial exercise of those powers. It is, then, the subject of fair inquiry how far such means may be employed.

The creation of a corporation, it is said, appertains to sovereignty. This is admitted. But to what portion of sovereignty does it appertain? Does it belong to one more than to another? In America, the powers of sovereignty are divided between the government of the Union and those of the states. They are each sovereign with respect to the objects committed to it, and neither sovereign with respect to the objects committed to the other.

We cannot comprehend that train of reasoning, which would maintain that the extent of power granted by the people is to be ascertained not by the nature and terms of the grant, but by its date. Some state constitutions were formed before, some since, that of the United States. We cannot believe that their relation to each other is in any degree dependent upon this circumstance. Their respective powers must, we think, be precisely the same as if they had been formed at the same time. Had they been formed at the same time, and had the people conferred on the General Government the power contained in the Constitution, and on the states the whole residuum of power, would it have been asserted that the government of the Union was not sovereign, with respect to those objects which were intrusted to it, in relation to which its laws were declared to be supreme?

- *There were thirteen states in 1787 when the Constitution was ratified. At the end of 1819, there were twenty-one states. What is Marshall saying about the way all states must think of the Constitution?*

If this could not have been asserted, we cannot well comprehend the process of reasoning which maintains that a power appertaining to sovereignty cannot be connected with that vast portion of it which is granted to the general government, so far as it is calculated to subserve the legitimate objects of that government. The power of creating a corporation, though appertaining to sovereignty, is not, like the power of making war or levying taxes or of regulating commerce, a great substantive and independent power which cannot be implied as incidental to other powers or used as a means of executing them. It is never the end for which other powers are exercised, but a means by which other objects are accomplished. No contributions are made to charity for the sake of an incorporation, but a corporation is created to administer the charity; no seminary of learning is instituted in order to be incorporated, but the corporate character is conferred to subserve the purposes of education. No city was ever built with the sole object of being incorporated, but is incorporated as affording the best means of being well governed. The power of creating a corporation is never used for its own sake, but for the purpose of effecting something else. No sufficient reason is therefore perceived why it may not pass as incidental to those powers which are expressly given if it be a direct mode of executing them.

But the Constitution of the United States has not left the right of Congress to employ the necessary means for the execution of the powers conferred on the government to general reasoning. To its enumeration of powers is added that of making "All laws which shall be necessary and proper for carrying into execution the foregoing powers, and all other powers vested by this Constitution in the government of the United States or in any department thereof."

The counsel for the State of Maryland have urged various arguments to prove that this clause, though in terms a grant of power, is not so in effect, but is really restrictive of the general right which might otherwise be implied of selecting means for executing the enumerated powers. In support of this proposition, they have found it necessary to contend that this clause was inserted for the purpose of conferring on Congress the power of making laws. That, without it, doubts might be entertained whether Congress could exercise its powers in the form of legislation.

But the argument on which most reliance is placed is drawn from that peculiar language of this clause. Congress is not empowered by it to make all laws which may have relation to the powers conferred on the Government, but such only as may be "necessary and proper" for carrying them into execution. The word "necessary" is considered as controlling the whole sentence, and as limiting the right to pass laws for the execution of the granted powers to such as are indispensable, and without which the power would be nugatory. That it excludes the choice of means, and leaves to Congress in each case that only which is most direct and simple.

Is it true that this is the sense in which the word "necessary" is always used? Does it always import an absolute physical necessity so strong that one thing to which another may be termed necessary cannot exist without that other? We think it does not. If reference be had to its use in the common affairs of the world or in approved authors, we find that it frequently imports no more than that one thing is convenient, or useful, or essential to another. To employ the means necessary to an end is generally understood as employing any means calculated to produce the end, and not as being confined to those single means without which the end would be entirely unattainable. Such is the character of human language that no word conveys to the mind in all situations one single definite idea, and nothing is more common than to use words in a figurative sense.

Almost all compositions contain words which, taken in their rigorous sense, would convey a meaning different from that which is obviously intended. It is essential to just construction that many words which import something excessive should be understood in a more mitigated sense—in that sense which common usage justifies. The word "necessary" is of this description. It has not a fixed character peculiar to itself. It admits of all degrees of comparison, and is often connected with other words which increase or diminish the impression the mind receives of the urgency it imports. A thing may be necessary, very necessary, absolutely or indispensably necessary. To no mind would the same idea be conveyed by these several phrases.

The comment on the word is well illustrated by the passage cited at the bar from the 10th section of the 1st article of the Constitution. It is, we think, impossible to compare the sentence which prohibits a state from laying "imposts, or duties on imports or exports, except what may be absolutely necessary for executing its inspection laws," with that which authorizes Congress "to make all laws which shall be necessary and proper for carrying into execution" the powers of the general government without feeling a conviction that the convention understood itself to change materially the meaning of the word "necessary," by prefixing the word "absolutely." This word, then, like others, is used in various senses, and, in its construction, the subject, the context, the intention of the person using them are all to be taken into view.

Let this be done in the case under consideration. The subject is the execution of those great powers on which the welfare of a nation essentially depends. It must have been the intention of those who gave these powers to insure, so far as human prudence could insure, their beneficial execution. This could not be done by confiding the choice of means to such narrow limits as not to leave it in the power of Congress to adopt any which might be appropriate, and which were conducive to the end. This provision is made in a Constitution intended to endure for ages to come, and consequently to be adapted to the various crises of human affairs. To have prescribed the means by which government should, in all future time, execute its powers would have been to change entirely the character of the instrument and give it the properties of a legal code. It would have been an unwise attempt to provide by immutable rules for exigencies which, if foreseen at all, must have been seen dimly, and which can be best provided for as they occur.

- *What is Marshall saying about the creators of the Constitution? What did they intend by including the "necessary and proper" clause?*

If we apply this principle of construction to any of the powers of the government, we shall find it so pernicious in its operation that we shall be compelled to discard it. The powers vested in Congress may certainly be carried into execution, without prescribing an oath of office. The power to exact this security for the faithful performance of duty is not given, nor is it indispensably necessary. The different departments may be established; taxes may be imposed and collected; armies and navies may be raised and maintained; and money may be borrowed, without requiring an oath of office. It might be argued with as much plausibility as other incidental powers have been assailed that the convention was not unmindful of this subject. The oath which might be exacted—that of fidelity to the Constitution—is prescribed, and no other can be required. Yet he would be charged with insanity who should contend that the legislature might not superadd to the oath directed by the Constitution such other oath of office as its wisdom might suggest.

Congress is empowered "to provide for the punishment of counterfeiting the securities and current coin of the United States," and "to define and punish piracies and felonies committed on the high seas, and offences against the law of nations." The several powers of Congress may exist in a very imperfect State, to be sure, but they may exist and be carried into execution, although no punishment should be inflicted, in cases where the right to punish is not expressly given.

In ascertaining the sense in which the word "necessary" is used in this clause of the Constitution, we may derive some aid from that with which it is associated. Congress shall have power "to make all laws which shall be necessary and proper to carry into execution" the powers of the government. If the word "necessary" was used in that strict and rigorous sense for which the counsel for the State of Maryland contend, it would be an extraordinary departure from the usual course of the human mind, as exhibited in composition, to add a word the only possible effect of which is to qualify that strict and rigorous meaning, to present to the mind the idea of some choice of means of legislation not strained and compressed within the narrow limits for which gentlemen contend.

We think so for the following reasons:

1. The clause is placed among the powers of Congress, not among the limitations on those powers.

2. Its terms purport to enlarge, not to diminish, the powers vested in the Government. It purports to be an additional power, not a restriction on those already granted. No reason has been or can be assigned for thus concealing an intention to narrow the discretion of the national legislature under words which purport to enlarge it.

The result of the most careful and attentive consideration bestowed upon this clause is that, if it does not enlarge, it cannot be construed to restrain, the powers of Congress, or to impair the right of the legislature to exercise its best judgment in the selection of measures to carry into execution the Constitutional powers of the government. If no other motive for its insertion can be suggested, a sufficient one is found in the desire to remove all doubts respecting the right to legislate on that vast mass of incidental powers which must be involved in the Constitution if that instrument be not a splendid bauble.

- *Marshall is indirectly saying that Daniel Webster (the attorney for the State of Maryland) is demeaning the Constitution. How does he convey this idea?*

We admit, as all must admit, that the powers of the government are limited, and that its limits are not to be transcended. But we think the sound construction of the Constitution must allow to the national legislature that discretion with respect to the means by which the powers it confers are to be carried into execution which will enable that body to perform the high duties assigned to it in the manner most beneficial to the people. Let the end be legitimate, let it be within the scope of the Constitution, and all means which are appropriate, which are plainly adapted to that end, which are not prohibited, but consist with the letter and spirit of the Constitution, are Constitutional.

After the most deliberate consideration, it is the unanimous and decided opinion of this Court that the act to incorporate the Bank of the United States is a law made in pursuance of the Constitution, and is a part of the supreme law of the land.

The branches, proceeding from the same stock and being conducive to the complete accomplishment of the object, are equally constitutional. It would have been unwise to locate them in the charter, and it would be unnecessarily inconvenient to employ the legislative power in making those subordinate arrangements. The great duties of the bank are prescribed; those duties require branches; and the bank itself may, we think, be safely trusted with the selection of places where those branches shall be fixed, reserving always to the government the right to require that a branch shall be located where it may be deemed necessary.

It being the opinion of the Court that the act incorporating the bank is constitutional, and that the power of establishing a branch in the State of Maryland might be properly exercised by the bank itself, we proceed to inquire:

2. Whether the State of Maryland may, without violating the Constitution, tax that branch?

That the power of taxation is one of vital importance; that it is retained by the states; that it is not abridged by the grant of a similar power to the Government of the Union; that it is to be concurrently exercised by the two Governments—are truths which have never been denied. But such is the paramount character of the Constitution that its capacity to withdraw any subject from the action of even this power is admitted. The states are expressly forbidden to lay any duties on imports or exports except what may be absolutely necessary for executing their inspection laws. If the obligation of this prohibition must be conceded—if it may restrain a state from the exercise of its taxing power on imports and exports—the same paramount character would seem to restrain, as it certainly may restrain, a State from such other exercise of this power as is in its nature incompatible with, and repugnant to, the constitutional laws of the Union. A law absolutely repugnant to another as entirely repeals that other as if express terms of repeal were used.

On this ground, the counsel for the bank place its claim to be exempted from the power of a state to tax its operations. There is no express provision for the case, but the claim has been sustained on a principle which so entirely pervades the Constitution, is so intermixed with the materials which compose it, so interwoven with its web, so blended with its texture, as to be incapable of being separated from it without rending it into shreds.

That the power of taxing it by the states may be exercised so as to destroy it is too obvious to be denied. But taxation is said to be an absolute power which acknowledges no other limits than those expressly prescribed in the Constitution, and, like sovereign power of every other description, is intrusted to the discretion of those who use it. But the very terms of this argument admit that the sovereignty of the state, in the article of taxation itself, is subordinate to, and may be controlled by, the Constitution of the United States. How far it has been controlled by that instrument must be a question of construction. In making this construction, no principle, not declared, can be admissible which would defeat the legitimate operations of a supreme government. It is of the very essence of supremacy to remove all obstacles to its action within its own sphere, and so to modify every power vested in subordinate governments as to exempt its own operations from their own influence. This effect need not be stated in terms. It is so involved in the declaration of supremacy, so necessarily implied in it, that the expression of it could not make it more certain. We must, therefore, keep it in view while construing the Constitution.

The argument on the part of the State of Maryland is not that the states may directly resist a law of Congress, but that they may exercise their acknowledged powers upon it, and that the Constitution leaves them this right, in the confidence that they will not abuse it. Before we proceed to examine this argument and to subject it to test of the Constitution, we must be permitted to bestow a few considerations on the nature and extent of this original right of taxation, which is acknowledged to remain with the states. It is admitted that the power of taxing the people and their property is essential to the very existence of government, and may be legitimately exercised on the objects to which it is applicable, to the utmost extent to which the government may choose to carry it. The only security against the abuse of this power is found in the structure of the government itself. In imposing a tax, the legislature acts upon its constituents. This is, in general, a sufficient security against erroneous and oppressive taxation.

The people of a state, therefore, give to their government a right of taxing themselves and their property, and as the exigencies of government cannot be limited, they prescribe no limits to the exercise of this right, resting confidently on the interest of the legislator and on the influence of the constituent over their representative to guard them against its abuse. But the means employed by the government of the Union have no such security, nor is the right of a state to tax them sustained by the same theory. Those means are not given by the people of a particular state, not given by the constituents of the legislature which claim the right to tax them, but by the people of all the states. They are given by all, for the benefit of all—and, upon theory, should be subjected to that government only which belongs to all.

- *Who is Marshall saying the State of Maryland is really taxing if they are allowed to tax a federal bank?*

If we measure the power of taxation residing in a state by the extent of sovereignty which the people of a single state possess and can confer on its government, we have an intelligible standard, applicable to every case to which the power may be applied. We have a principle which leaves the power of taxing the people and property of a state unimpaired; which leaves to a state the command of all its resources, and which places beyond its reach all those powers which are conferred by the people of the United States on the government of the Union, and all those means which are given for the purpose of carrying those powers into execution. We have a principle which is safe for the states and safe for the Union. We are relieved, as we ought to be, from clashing sovereignty; from interfering powers; from a repugnancy between a right in one government to pull down what there is an acknowledged right in another to build up; from the incompatibility of a right in one government to destroy what there is a right in another to preserve. We are not driven to the perplexing inquiry, so unfit for the judicial department, what degree of taxation is the legitimate use and what degree may amount to the abuse of the power. The attempt to use it on the means employed by the government of the Union, in pursuance of the Constitution, is itself an abuse because it is the usurpation of a power which the people of a single state cannot give.

- *What is Marshall arguing regarding the limitations of a state's right regarding people from another state? Do you find this argument convincing?*

We find, then, on just theory, a total failure of this original right to tax the means employed by the government of the Union, for the execution of its powers. The right never existed, and the question whether it has been surrendered cannot arise.

If we apply the principle for which the State of Maryland contends, to the Constitution generally, we shall find it capable of changing totally the character of that instrument. We shall find it capable of arresting all the measures of the government, and of prostrating it at the foot of the states. The American people have declared their Constitution and the laws made in pursuance thereof to be supreme, but this principle would transfer the supremacy, in fact, to the states.

If the states may tax one instrument, employed by the government in the execution of its powers, they may tax any and every other instrument. They may tax the mail; they may tax the mint; they may tax patent rights; they may tax the papers of the custom house; they may tax judicial process; they may tax all the means employed by the government to an excess which would defeat all the ends of government. This was not intended by the American people. They did not design to make their government dependent on the states.

- *Why do you think Marshall listed all of the other federal activities that a state could tax if the Maryland tax was held to be constitutional?*

The Court has bestowed on this subject its most deliberate consideration. The result is a conviction that the states have no power, by taxation or otherwise, to retard, impede, burden, or in any manner control the operations of the constitutional laws enacted by Congress to carry into execution the powers vested in the general government. This is, we think, the unavoidable consequence of that supremacy which the Constitution has declared.

We are unanimously of opinion that the law passed by the Legislature of Maryland, imposing a tax on the Bank of the United States is unconstitutional and void.

This opinion does not deprive the states of any resources which they originally possessed. It does not extend to a tax paid by the real property of the bank, in common with the other real property within the state, nor to a tax imposed on the interest which the citizens of Maryland may hold in this institution, in common with other property of the same description throughout the state. But this is a tax on the operations of the bank, and is, consequently, a tax on the operation of an instrument employed by the government of the Union to carry its powers into execution. Such a tax must be unconstitutional.

Connecting, Arguing, and Analyzing the Case

1. How would the writer of Brutus No. 1 have reacted to the Court's decision in *McCulloch v. Maryland*?

2. Read the opinion in the case *State of Missouri v. Holland*, 252 U.S. 416 (1920), where the Court used the "necessary and proper" clause to rule against a Tenth Amendment challenge to treaty powers of the United States. Do you agree with the Court's reasoning?
3. In the opinion, Justice Marshall spends a great deal of time discussing the "necessary" portion of the "necessary and proper" clause. The case *Printz v. United States*, 521 U.S. 898 (1997), also deals with the "necessary and proper" clause but focuses more on the issue of "proper." Read the case and then discuss why something could be necessary but not proper under the Constitution.
4. *National Federation of Independent Business v. Sebelius*, 567 U.S. 519 (2012) found the Court ruling on the legality of the "individual mandate" portion of the Affordable Care Act, more commonly known as Obamacare. Chief Justice Roberts wrote that Congress did not have the right to regulate "inactivity," in other words, a tax penalty for failure to enroll in an insurance program, by using either the "necessary and proper" clause or the Commerce Clause. Read the case *United States v. Lopez* in chapter 13, and using Justice Rehnquist's articulation of the three areas Congress can regulate under the Commerce Clause, write an argument challenging the *National Federation of Independent Business v. Sebelius* decision using *both* the "necessary and proper" clause and the Commerce Clause to support your argument.

Chapter Three

Schenck v. United States

The First Amendment of the Constitution states, "Congress shall make no law respecting an establishment of religion, or prohibiting the free exercise thereof; or abridging the freedom of speech, or of the press; or the right of the people peaceably to assemble, and to petition the Government for a redress of grievances." After entering World War I in 1917, Congress passed the Espionage Act, which made it illegal to "willfully make or convey false reports or false statements with intent to interfere with the operation or success of the military or naval forces of the United States or to promote the success of its enemies . . . [or] willfully cause or attempt to cause insubordination, disloyalty, mutiny, or refusal of duty, in the military or naval forces of the United States, or shall willfully obstruct the recruiting or enlistment service of the United States, to the injury of the service or of the United States" to protect efforts to enlist and draft men in the armed services.

The petitioner was the general secretary of the U.S. Socialist Party, which opposed the registration for selective service. On behalf of his organization, he printed and distributed fifteen thousand leaflets calling for people to refuse to submit to the draft. He was found guilty on three counts of violating the Espionage Act and sentenced to thirty years in prison. He appealed, stating the Espionage Act violated his First Amendment right to freedom of speech.

Legal Issue

Did the provisions in the Espionage Act of 1917 violate the petitioner's First Amendment right to freedom of speech?

Vocabulary

Conscription: compulsory enrollment of persons especially for military service
Averment: the act of declaring positively
Substantive: considerable in amount or numbers
Obstructive: hindering from passage, action, or operation; impeding
Disparage: to lower in honor or esteem

Parties in this Case

Petitioner: Charles T. Schenck
Respondent: The U.S. government
Edited version of case in the original language with distractors removed.

SCHENCK V. UNITED STATES, 249 U.S. 47 (1919)

MR. JUSTICE HOLMES delivered the opinion of the court.
    This is an indictment in three counts. The first charges a conspiracy to violate the Espionage Act of June 15, 1917, by causing and attempting to cause insubordination in the military and naval forces of the United States, and to obstruct the recruiting and enlistment service of the United States, when the United States was at war with the German Empire that the defendants willfully conspired to have printed and circulated to men who had been called and accepted for military service under the Act of May 18, 1917, a document set forth and alleged to be calculated to cause such insubordination and obstruction. The count alleges overt acts in pursuance of the conspiracy, ending in the distribution of the document set forth. The second count alleges a conspiracy to commit an offence against the United States to use the mails for the transmission of matter declared to be nonmailable of the Act of June 15, 1917, the above mentioned document, with an averment of the same overt acts. The third count charges an unlawful use of the mails for the transmission of the same matter and otherwise as above. The defendants were found guilty on all the counts. They set up the First Amendment to the Constitution forbidding Congress to make any law abridging the freedom of speech, or of the press.
    It is argued that the evidence, if admissible, was not sufficient to prove that the defendant Schenck was concerned in sending the documents. According to the testimony, Schenck said he was general secretary of the Socialist party, and had charge of the Socialist headquarters from which the documents were sent. He identified a book found there as the minutes of the Executive Committee of the party. The book showed a resolution of August 13, 1917, that 15,000 leaflets should be printed on the other side of one of

them in use, to be mailed to men who had passed exemption boards, and for distribution. Schenck personally attended to the printing. On August 20, the general secretary's report said "Obtained new leaflets from printer and started work addressing envelopes" and there was a resolve that Comrade Schenck be allowed $125 for sending leaflets through the mail. He said that he had about fifteen or sixteen thousand printed. There were files of the circular in question in the inner office which he said were printed on the other side of the one sided circular, and were there for distribution. Other copies were proved to have been sent through the mails to drafted men. Without going into confirmatory details that were proved, no reasonable man could doubt that the defendant Schenck was largely instrumental in sending the circulars about. The argument as to the sufficiency of the evidence that the defendants conspired to send the documents only impairs the seriousness of the real defence.

It is objected that the documentary evidence was not admissible because obtained upon a search warrant, valid so far as appears. The contrary is established. The search warrant did not issue against the defendant, but against the Socialist headquarters at 1326 Arch Street, and it would seem that the documents technically were not even in the defendants' possession. Notwithstanding some protest in argument, the notion that evidence even directly proceeding from the defendant in a criminal proceeding is excluded in all cases by the Fifth Amendment is plainly unsound.

- *Why is it important that the Fifth Amendment issues be addressed before the court considers the First Amendment issues? Why would a due process argument stop the case?*

The document in question, upon its first printed side, recited the first section of the Thirteenth Amendment, said that the idea embodied in it was violated by the Conscription Act, and that a conscript is little better than a convict.

- *What argument would Schenk have that utilizes the Thirteenth Amendment when it comes to the draft? Do you agree with that argument?*

In impassioned language, it intimated that conscription was despotism in its worst form, and a monstrous wrong against humanity in the interest of Wall Street's chosen few. It said "Do not submit to intimidation," but in form, at least, confined itself to peaceful measures such as a petition for the repeal of the act. The other and later printed side of the sheet was headed "Assert Your Rights." It stated reasons for alleging that anyone violated the Constitution when he refused to recognize "your right to assert your opposition to the draft," and went on "If you do not assert and support your rights, you are helping to deny or disparage rights which it is the solemn duty of all citizens and residents of the United States to retain."

It described the arguments on the other side as coming from cunning politicians and a mercenary capitalist press, and even silent consent to the conscription law as helping to support an infamous conspiracy. It denied the power to send our citizens away to foreign shores to shoot up the people of other lands, and added that words could not express the condemnation such cold-blooded ruthlessness deserves, winding up, "You must do your share to maintain, support and uphold the rights of the people of this country."

- *What events in recent American history could be similar to the mailings sent by Schenk and the Socialists?*

Of course, the document would not have been sent unless it had been intended to have some effect, and we do not see what effect it could be expected to have upon persons subject to the draft except to influence them to obstruct the carrying of it out. The defendants do not deny that the jury might find against them on this point.

But it is said, suppose that that was the tendency of this circular, it is protected by the First Amendment to the Constitution. Two of the strongest expressions are said to be quoted respectively from well known public men. It well may be that the prohibition of laws abridging the freedom of speech is not confined to previous restraints, although to prevent them may have been the main purpose. We admit that, in many places and in ordinary times, the defendants, in saying all that was said in the circular, would have been within their constitutional rights. But the character of every act depends upon the circumstances in which it is done.

- *Why does the Court think it is important to distinguish that the speech that Schenck made might have been fine during a different time? What is at stake for the country? Do you agree with this argument?*

The most stringent protection of free speech would not protect a man in falsely shouting fire in a theatre and causing a panic. It does not even protect a man from an injunction against uttering words that may have all the effect of force. The question in every case is whether the words used are used in such circumstances and are of such a nature as to create a clear and present danger that they will bring about the substantive evils that Congress has a right to prevent. It is a question of proximity and degree.

- *Justice Holmes's statement about "shouting fire in a theatre" is one of the most quoted phrases from cases that limit the First Amendment. What other phrases do you know of that people cannot say because they might present "a clear and present danger"? Where do you think the line should be drawn between speech and other interests?*

When a nation is at war, many things that might be said in time of peace are such a hindrance to its effort that their utterance will not be endured so long as men fight, and that no Court could regard them as protected by any constitutional right. It seems to be admitted that, if an actual obstruction of the recruiting service were proved, liability for words that produced that effect might be enforced. The statute of 1917 punishes conspiracies to obstruct, as well as actual obstruction. If the act (speaking, or circulating a paper), its tendency, and the intent with which it is done are the same, we perceive no ground for saying that success alone warrants making the act a crime. Indeed, that case might be said to dispose of the present contention if the precedent covers all media concludendi. But, as the right to free speech was not referred to specially, we have thought fit to add a few words.

- *Why does the Court think it is enough to have proved the conspiracy, rather than to prove that someone was actually deterred by the flyers?*

It was not argued that a conspiracy to obstruct the draft was not within the words of the Act of 1917. The words are "obstruct the recruiting or enlistment service," and it might be suggested that they refer only to making it hard to get volunteers. Recruiting heretofore usually having been accomplished by getting volunteers, the word is apt to call up that method only in our minds. But recruiting is gaining fresh supplies for the forces, as well by draft as otherwise.
Judgments affirmed.

Connecting, Arguing, and Analyzing the Case

1. President Woodrow Wilson had only wanted those fighting in World War I to be volunteers, yet six weeks after entering the war, less than seventy-five thousand men had enlisted when Wilson had wanted an army of one million men. Research the success of the draft and recruiting efforts after the Espionage Act of 1917 was instituted. Was this limit of free speech successful in the effort to retain soldiers?
2. Create a Likert Scale where you balance the rights of the individual and the needs of society. Where should the line be drawn between them?
3. *Brandenburg v. Ohio*, 395 U.S. 444 (1969), took the Court away from the "clear and present danger" test to the "imminent lawless action" test for restricting speech. In his concurrence, Justice William O. Douglas referred to the *Schenck* case and the misuse of the "clear and

present danger" test that he said had likely prevented legitimate First Amendment claims from coming to the Court. Research *Brandenburg*'s test and write a brief argument articulating why the "clear and present danger" is not as effective in preserving an individual's constitutional rights.

Chapter Four

Brown v. Board of Education of Topeka

Prior to the landmark decision of *Brown v. Board of Education*, public schools in the United States typically separated students by race. Instead of students attending their neighborhood school, as is common in many communities today, many African American students were bused, sometimes hours, to a school for students of the same race. A U.S. Supreme Court decision, *Plessy v. Ferguson*, seemed to permit this separation as the Court allowed segregation on public transportation. However, as the nation evolved and more African American children were attending school (prior to the Civil War, many were entirely uneducated), the Court faced the need to reconsider its decision in *Plessy*. At issue was whether public schools separated by race could actually be "separate but equal" in reality. Could teachers be of the same quality? Would facilities be comparable? And would the opportunity for education separate, rather than together, ever be considered equal?

Legal Issue

Are segregated public schools allowed under the Equal Protection Clause of the Fourteenth Amendment of the U.S. Constitution?

Vocabulary

Segregation: The separation of individuals or groups of people from one another
Separate but Equal: A legal concept set forth in *Plessy v. Ferguson* that facilities can be segregated but must provide equal opportunity

Parties in the Case

Petitioner: Linda Brown (a minor student) along with other students from South Carolina, Virginia, and Delaware (all of whom had similar challenges to laws segregating schools in their states)
Respondent: The Board of Education of Topeka, Kansas
 Edited version of case in the original language with distractors removed.

BROWN V. BOARD OF EDUCATION OF TOPEKA,
347 U.S. 483 (1954)

MR. CHIEF JUSTICE WARREN delivered the opinion of the Court.
[1]
These cases come to us from the states of Kansas, South Carolina, Virginia, and Delaware. They are premised on different facts and different local conditions, but a common legal question justifies their consideration together in this consolidated opinion.

In each of the cases, minors of the Negro race, through their legal representatives, seek the aid of the courts in obtaining admission to the public schools of their community on a non-segregated basis. In each instance, they had been denied admission to schools attended by white children under laws requiring or permitting segregation according to race. This segregation was alleged to deprive the plaintiffs of the equal protection of the laws under the Fourteenth Amendment. In each of the cases other than the Delaware case, a three-judge federal district court denied relief to the plaintiffs on the so-called "separate but equal" doctrine announced by this Court in *Plessy v. Ferguson*, 163 U.S. 537. Under that doctrine, equality of treatment is accorded when the races are provided substantially equal facilities, even though these facilities be separate. In the Delaware case, the Supreme Court of Delaware adhered to that doctrine, but ordered that the plaintiffs be admitted to the white schools because of their superiority to the Negro schools.

- Plessy v. Ferguson *permitted "separate but equal" on public transportation (railcars). Why do you think the Court is reconsidering its own decision here when the issue moved to public schools? Why might the setting of a public school cause the Court to reconsider?*

The plaintiffs contend that segregated public schools are not "equal" and cannot be made "equal," and that hence they are deprived of the equal protection of the laws. Because of the obvious importance of the question presented, the Court took jurisdiction. Argument was heard in the 1952 Term, and reargument was heard this Term on certain questions propounded by the Court.

[2]
Reargument was largely devoted to the circumstances surrounding the adoption of the Fourteenth Amendment in 1868. It covered exhaustively consideration of the Amendment in Congress, ratification by the states, then existing practices in racial segregation, and the views of proponents and opponents of the Amendment.

- *The Fourteenth Amendment was adopted after the Civil War and has been used to protect the rights of citizens under state and federal laws. What does the Fourteenth Amendment say and how does it apply to public schools?*

This discussion and our own investigation convince us that, although these sources cast some light, it is not enough to resolve the problem with which we are faced. At best, they are inconclusive. The most avid proponents of the post-War Amendments undoubtedly intended them to remove all legal distinctions among "all persons born or naturalized in the United States." Their opponents, just as certainly, were antagonistic to both the letter and the spirit of the Amendments and wished them to have the most limited effect. What others in Congress and the state legislatures had in mind cannot be determined with any degree of certainty.

An additional reason for the inconclusive nature of the Amendment's history, with respect to segregated schools, is the status of public education at that time. In the South, the movement toward free common schools, supported by general taxation, had not yet taken hold. Education of white children was largely in the hands of private groups. Education of Negroes was almost nonexistent, and practically all of the race were illiterate. In fact, any education of Negroes was forbidden by law in some states. Today, in contrast, many Negroes have achieved outstanding success in the arts and sciences as well as in the business and professional world. It is true that public school education at the time of the Amendment had advanced further in the North, but the effect of the Amendment on Northern States was generally ignored in the congressional debates. Even in the North, the conditions of public education did not approximate those existing today. The curriculum was usually rudimentary; ungraded schools were common in rural areas; the school term was but three months a year in many states; and compulsory school attendance was virtually unknown. As a consequence, it is not surprising that there should be so little in the history of the Fourteenth Amendment relating to its intended effect on public education.

- *How did the country change after the Fourteenth Amendment? Do you think these were anticipated or unanticipated results of the amendment?*

In the first cases in this Court construing the Fourteenth Amendment, decided shortly after its adoption, the Court interpreted it as proscribing all state-imposed discriminations against the Negro race. The doctrine of "separate but equal" did not make its appearance in this Court until 1896 in the case of *Plessy v. Ferguson*, involving not education but transportation. American courts have since labored with the doctrine for over half a century. In this Court, there have been six cases involving the "separate but equal" doctrine in the field of public education. In more recent cases, all on the graduate school level, inequality was found in that specific benefits enjoyed by white students were denied to Negro students of the same educational qualifications. In none of these cases was it necessary to re-examine the doctrine to grant relief to the Negro plaintiff. And in *Sweatt v. Painter*, the Court expressly reserved decision on the question whether *Plessy v. Ferguson* should be held inapplicable to public education.

In the instant cases, that question is directly presented. Here, unlike *Sweatt v. Painter*, there are findings below that the Negro and white schools involved have been equalized, or are being equalized, with respect to buildings, curricula, qualifications and salaries of teachers, and other "tangible" factors. Our decision, therefore, cannot turn on merely a comparison of these tangible factors in the Negro and white schools involved in each of the cases. We must look instead to the effect of segregation itself on public education.

- *If the schools had truly been separate and equal, could the Court have stopped here and issued a ruling? Why or why not?*

[3]
In approaching this problem, we cannot turn the clock back to 1868 when the Amendment was adopted, or even to 1896 when *Plessy v. Ferguson* was written. We must consider public education in the light of its full development and its present place in American life throughout the Nation. Only in this way can it be determined if segregation in public schools deprives these plaintiffs of the equal protection of the laws.

- *Why does the Court want to consider the "place" of education in American life? If you had to describe its place, what would you say?*

[4]
Today, education is perhaps the most important function of state and local governments. Compulsory school attendance laws and the great expenditures for education both demonstrate our recognition of the importance of education to our democratic society. It is required in the performance of our most basic public responsibilities, even service in the armed forces. It is the very foundation of good citizenship. Today it is a principal instrument in awaken-

ing the child to cultural values, in preparing him for later professional training, and in helping him to adjust normally to his environment. In these days, it is doubtful that any child may reasonably be expected to succeed in life if he is denied the opportunity of an education. Such an opportunity, where the state has undertaken to provide it, is a right which must be made available to all on equal terms.

- *The Court seems to place a great deal of weight on the importance of public school education. Why?*

[5]
We come then to the question presented: Does segregation of children in public schools solely on the basis of race, even though the physical facilities and other "tangible" factors may be equal, deprive the children of the minority group of equal educational opportunities? We believe that it does.

In *Sweatt v. Painter*, in finding that a segregated law school for Negroes could not provide them equal educational opportunities, this Court relied in large part on "those qualities which are incapable of objective measurement but which make for greatness in a law school." In *McLaurin v. Oklahoma State Regents*, the Court, in requiring that a Negro admitted to a white graduate school be treated like all other students, again resorted to intangible considerations: ". . . his ability to study, to engage in discussions and exchange views with other students, and, in general, to learn his profession." Such considerations apply with added force to children in grade and high schools. To separate them from others of similar age and qualifications solely because of their race generates a feeling of inferiority as to their status in the community that may affect their hearts and minds in a way unlikely ever to be undone. The effect of this separation on their educational opportunities was well stated by a finding in the Kansas case by a court which nevertheless felt compelled to rule against the Negro plaintiffs:

> Segregation of white and colored children in public schools has a detrimental effect upon the colored children. The impact is greater when it has the sanction of the law; for the policy of separating the races is usually interpreted as denoting the inferiority of the negro group. A sense of inferiority affects the motivation of a child to learn. Segregation with the sanction of law, therefore, has a tendency to [retard] the educational and mental development of negro children and to deprive them of some of the benefits they would receive in a racial[ly] integrated school system.

Whatever may have been the extent of psychological knowledge at the time of *Plessy v. Ferguson*, this finding is amply supported by modern authority. Any language in *Plessy v. Ferguson* contrary to this finding is rejected.

- *Why does the Court seem to think that public K–12 education is arguably more important than graduate school education?*

[6]

We conclude that in the field of public education the doctrine of "separate but equal" has no place. Separate educational facilities are inherently unequal. Therefore, we hold that the plaintiffs and others similarly situated for whom the actions have been brought are, by reason of the segregation complained of, deprived of the equal protection of the laws guaranteed by the Fourteenth Amendment. This disposition makes unnecessary any discussion whether such segregation also violates the Due Process Clause of the Fourteenth Amendment.

Because these are class actions, because of the wide applicability of this decision, and because of the great variety of local conditions, the formulation of decrees in these cases presents problems of considerable complexity. On reargument, the consideration of appropriate relief was necessarily subordinated to the primary question—the constitutionality of segregation in public education. We have now announced that such segregation is a denial of the equal protection of the laws. In order that we may have the full assistance of the parties in formulating decrees, the cases will be restored to the docket, and the parties are requested to present further argument on Questions 4 and 5 previously propounded by the Court for the reargument this Term. The Attorney General of the United States is again invited to participate. The Attorneys General of the states requiring or permitting segregation in public education will also be permitted to appear as *amici curiae* upon request to do so by September 15, 1954, and submission of briefs by October 1, 1954.

It is so ordered.

Connecting, Arguing, and Analyzing the Case

1. Many communities are moving toward single-sex education (all-boys schools or all-girls schools) in order to better educate girls and/or boys in single-sex environments. Some research supports that students learn better in these scenarios, while others think this is a more modern form of segregation. Is this type of separation constitutional under *Brown v. Board of Education*? Why or why not?
2. In this case, Linda Brown and her sister had to walk through a railyard and board a bus to attend the all-black school in her town. What if the all-black school was in Linda's neighborhood next door to the all-white school? Would that make the rationale of this case any different?
3. In 2016, reports emerged that U.S. public schools are in actuality still segregated, surprisingly not due to legal restrictions but due to soci-

oeconomic factors, neighborhood demographics, and poverty rates. Read "Evenness vs. Isolation in Schools" from *U.S. News and World Report*: https://www.usnews.com/news/education-news/articles/2018-06-25/the-complicated-facts-of-modern-school-segregation. Consider this information in light of *Missouri v. Jenkins*, a 1976 U.S. Supreme Court case that permitted "de facto" segregation (that is, segregation that naturally occurs and is not caused by enforcing a law) and distinguished that from "de jure" segregation (segregation that is caused by enforcing a law). Does de facto segregation hinder progress after the *Brown* decision?

4. Should legislative measure be taken to overcome the obstacles of today's naturally segregated schools? If so, how? Read "Segregation Is Not a Myth" by Will Stancil from *The Atlantic* here: https://www.theatlantic.com/education/archive/2018/03/school-segregation-is-not-a-myth/555614/. What arguments can you construct for and against segregation as it emerges in today's schools? Are your arguments constitutional under *Brown*?

Chapter Five

Baker v. Carr

The importance of a citizen's representation in state and local government is a vital component of a working democracy. In this early 1960s case, citizens of the state of Tennessee filed suit against the elected officials in charge of laying out the voting districts in the state. Prior to 1901, the law in Tennessee required a review of the number of state legislators assigned to a region based on the most recent census data collected every ten years.

In 1901, Tennessee changed this law to require use of the Federal Census data from 1900 to assign legislative positions to districts, and it was not revisited again until this case, nearly sixty years later. During those sixty years, the population of Tennessee changed, people migrated to larger cities, and the population of towns used in the 1900 Census had drastically changed, leaving the population of some larger cities with less representation per person than those that resided in small towns.

This case was brought under the Equal Protection Clause of the Fourteenth Amendment, which guarantees equal protection for all citizens under state and federal law. However, the Court had to first determine whether this was even a matter for the Court to decide—was it too political and did it thus need to be handled by the legislative body or Congress, or could the Court simply look at the rights of the voters and determine if they were equally treated under the law being used to assign legislative representation in the state?

Legal Issue

Do federal courts have the right to hear cases about the allotment of state legislative seats under the Equal Protection Clause of the Fourteenth Amendment, or is that a political matter reserved only for legislative bodies to resolve?

Vocabulary

Subject matter jurisdiction: The authority of a court to hear a case on a particular issue. The U.S. Supreme Court typically hears cases based on one of two reasons: the case involves a federal statute or challenge to the Constitution (federal question jurisdiction) or the case involves citizens of two different states and an amount in dispute of over $75,000 (diversity jurisdiction).
Debasement: "to lower in status, esteem, quality, or character" (Merriam-Webster)
Injunction: an order issued by a court to require a person or entity to refrain from doing something.
Apportionment: the allotment or assignment of legislators within a state
Cognizable: capable of being heard by a court
Standing: A party's ability to demonstrate sufficient harm or reason to be involved in a case to be heard by a court. If a party lacks standing, they are not close enough to the case to be heard.
Nonjusticiability: refers to a case that a court is not allowed to hear (because it is beyond their jurisdiction or reach)
Justiciable: refers to a case a court is allowed to hear because it is within the reach of the court's review
Enumeration: listing the number, or amount, of something

Parties in this Case

Petitioner: Charles Baker (an eligible voter in Memphis suing for himself and on behalf of other voters like him)
Respondent: James Carr (Tennessee Secretary of State)
Edited version of case in the original language with distractors removed.

BAKER V. CARR, 369 U.S. 186 (1962)

MR. JUSTICE BRENNAN delivered the opinion of the Court.

The General Assembly of Tennessee consists of the Senate, with 33 members, and the House of Representatives, with 99 members . . . Tennessee's standard for allocating legislative representation among her counties is the total number of qualified voters resident in the respective counties, subject only to minor qualifications. Decennial reapportionment in compliance with the constitutional scheme was effected by the General Assembly each decade from 1871 to 1901. In 1901, the General Assembly abandoned separate enumeration in favor of reliance upon the Federal Census, and passed the Apportionment Act here in controversy. In the more than 60 years since that action, all proposals in both Houses of the General Assembly for reapportionment have failed to pass.

- *The Apportionment Act basically replaced the requirement that district voting boundaries be redrawn based on the most recent census. This Act permitted these lines to be drawn based on the 1900 Federal Census and those lines remained in place until this case was brought in the early 1960s. How do you think the population of a state and where people live can change over that amount of time and why?*

Between 1901 and 1961, Tennessee has experienced substantial growth and redistribution of her population. In 1901, the population was 2,020,616, of whom 487,380 were eligible to vote. The 1960 Federal Census reports the State's population at 3,567,089, of whom 2,092,891 are eligible to vote. The relative standings of the counties in terms of qualified voters have changed significantly. It is primarily the continued application of the 1901 Apportionment Act to this shifted and enlarged voting population which gives rise to the present controversy.

Indeed, the complaint alleges that the 1901 statute, even as of the time of its passage, made no apportionment of Representatives and Senators in accordance with the constitutional formula, but instead arbitrarily and capriciously apportioned representatives in the Senate and House without reference to any logical or reasonable formula whatever.

It is further alleged that, "because of the population changes since 1900, and the failure of the Legislature to reapportion itself since 1901," the 1901 statute became "unconstitutional and obsolete." The complaint concludes that these plaintiffs and others similarly situated, are denied the equal protection of the laws accorded them by the Fourteenth Amendment to the Constitution of the United States by virtue of the debasement of their votes. They seek a declaration that the 1901 statute is unconstitutional and an injunction restraining the appellees from acting to conduct any further elections under it.

I
The District Court's Opinion and Order of Dismissal

Because we deal with this case on appeal from an order of dismissal granted on appellees' motions, precise identification of the issues presently confronting us demands clear exposition of the grounds upon which the District Court rested in dismissing the case. The dismissal order recited that the court sustained the appellees' grounds "(1) that the Court lacks jurisdiction of the subject matter, and (2) that the complaint fails to state a claim upon which relief can be granted."

- *To hear a case, a court must have "jurisdiction" or the proper authority to review the case and the party bringing the case to court must rely on (or suggest) an appropriate law on which a decision can be issued. Without these two conditions being met, a court is not permitted to hear a case that is brought before it. Does this case meet those conditions to be heard by the Court?*

We treat the first ground of dismissal as "lack of jurisdiction of the subject matter." The second we consider to result in a failure to state a justiciable cause of action.

The action is presently before the Court upon the defendants' motion to dismiss predicated upon three grounds: first, that the Court lacks jurisdiction of the subject matter; second, that the complaints fail to state a claim upon which relief can be granted, and third, that indispensable party defendants are not before the Court. The court proceeded to explain its action as turning on the case's presenting a "question of the distribution of political strength for legislative purposes." For, from a review of [numerous Supreme Court] . . . decisions, there can be no doubt that the federal rule, as enunciated and applied by the Supreme Court, is that the federal courts, whether from a lack of jurisdiction or from the inappropriateness of the subject matter for judicial consideration, will not intervene in cases of this type to compel legislative reapportionment. The Court went on to express doubts as to the feasibility of the various possible remedies sought by the plaintiffs. Then it made clear that its dismissal reflected a view not of doubt that violation of constitutional rights was alleged, but of a court's impotence to correct that violation:

- *Why might the lower court have reasoned that interfering in political issues, like the drawing of political districts, would be an overreach of its powers?*

With the plaintiffs' argument that the legislature of Tennessee is guilty of a clear violation of the state constitution and of the rights of the plaintiffs the Court entirely agrees. It also agrees that the evil is a serious one which should be corrected without further delay. But even so, the remedy in this situation clearly does not lie with the courts. It has long been recognized and is accepted doctrine that there are indeed some rights guaranteed by the Constitution for the violation of which the courts cannot give redress.

In light of the District Court's treatment of the case, we hold today only (a) that the court possessed jurisdiction of the subject matter; (b) that a justiciable cause of action is stated upon which appellants would be entitled to appropriate relief, and (c) because appellees raise the issue before this Court, that the appellants have standing to challenge the Tennessee apportionment statutes. Beyond noting that we have no cause at this stage to doubt the District Court will be able to fashion relief if violations of constitutional rights are found, it is improper now to consider what remedy would be most appropriate if appellants prevail at the trial.

- *The Court provides three reasons for reversing the lower court's resistance to address this case. What are those three reasons?*

II
Jurisdiction of the Subject Matter

The District Court was uncertain whether our cases withholding federal judicial relief rested upon a lack of federal jurisdiction or upon the inappropriateness of the subject matter for judicial consideration—what we have designated "nonjusticiability." Our conclusion, that this cause presents no nonjusticiable "political question" settles the only possible doubt that it is a case or controversy. Under the present heading of "Jurisdiction of the Subject Matter," we hold only that the matter set forth in the complaint does arise under the Constitution, and is within 28 U.S.C. § 1343.

Article III, 2, of the Federal Constitution provides that "The judicial Power shall extend to all Cases, in Law and Equity, arising under this Constitution, the Laws of the United States, and Treaties made, or which shall be made, under their Authority."

It is clear that the cause of action is one which "arises under" the Federal Constitution. The complaint alleges that the 1901 statute effects an apportionment that deprives the appellants of the equal protection of the laws in violation of the Fourteenth Amendment. Dismissal of the complaint upon the ground of lack of jurisdiction of the subject matter would, therefore, be justified only if that claim were "so attenuated and unsubstantial as to be absolutely devoid of merit," or "frivolous." That the claim is unsubstantial must be "very plain." Since the District Court obviously and correctly did not deem the asserted federal constitutional claim unsubstantial and frivolous, it should not have dismissed the complaint for want of jurisdiction of the subject matter.

Since the complaint plainly sets forth a case arising under the Constitution, the subject matter is within the federal judicial power defined in Art. III, § 2, and so within the power of Congress to assign to the jurisdiction of the District Courts. Congress has exercised that power in 28 U.S.C. § 1343(3): The district courts shall have original jurisdiction of any civil action authorized by law to be commenced by any person . . . [t]o redress the deprivation, under color of any State law, statute, ordinance, regulation, custom or usage, of any right, privilege or immunity secured by the Constitution of the United States.

An unbroken line of our precedents sustains the federal courts' jurisdiction of the subject matter of federal constitutional claims of this nature. The appellees refer to *Colegrove v. Green*, as authority that the District Court lacked jurisdiction of the subject matter.

Colegrove v. Green *was an earlier U.S. Supreme Court case that essentially said the courts had no right to interfere with legislative matters. That is, the two branches (legislative and judiciary) function separately and neither should arbitrarily interfere with the business of the other branch. In that case, the Court noted that only the U.S. Congress could determine if fair representation was provided by the states, not the judicial system. Why is this case different?*

Appellees misconceive the holding of that case. The holding was precisely contrary to their reading of it. Seven members of the Court participated in the decision. Unlike many other cases in this field which have assumed without discussion that there was jurisdiction, all three opinions filed in *Colegrove* discussed the question. Two of the opinions expressing the views of four of the Justices, a majority, flatly held that there was jurisdiction of the subject matter.

We hold that the District Court has jurisdiction of the subject matter of the federal constitutional claim asserted in the complaint.

III
Standing

A federal court cannot pronounce any statute, either of a State or of the United States, void, because irreconcilable with the Constitution, except as it is called upon to adjudge the legal rights of litigants in actual controversies.

- *What allowed the litigants in this case to have "standing" or the ability to be an active party to a case?*

Have the appellants alleged such a personal stake in the outcome of the controversy as to assure that concrete adverseness which sharpens the presentation of issues upon which the court so largely depends for illumination of difficult constitutional questions? This is the gist of the question of standing. It is, of course, a question of federal law.

The complaint was filed by residents of Davidson, Hamilton, Knox, Montgomery, and Shelby Counties. Each is a person allegedly qualified to vote for members of the General Assembly representing his county. These appellants sued on their own behalf and on behalf of all qualified voters of their respective counties, and further, on behalf of all voters of the State of Tennessee who are similarly situated.

The appellees are the Tennessee Secretary of State, Attorney General, Coordinator of Elections, and members of the State Board of Elections; the members of the State Board are sued in their own right and also as representatives of the County Election Commissioners whom they appoint.

We hold that the appellants do have standing to maintain this suit. Our decisions plainly support this conclusion. And *Colegrove v. Green*, squarely held that voters who allege facts showing disadvantage to themselves as individuals have standing to sue. These appellants seek relief in order to protect or vindicate an interest of their own, and of those similarly situated. Their constitutional claim is, in substance, that the 1901 statute constitutes arbitrary and capricious state action, offensive to the Fourteenth Amendment in its irrational disregard of the standard of apportionment prescribed by the State's Constitution or of any standard, effecting a gross disproportion of representation to voting population. The injury which appellants assert is that this classification disfavors the voters in the counties in which they reside, placing them in a position of constitutionally unjustifiable inequality *vis-a-vis* voters in irrationally favored counties. A citizen's right to a vote free of arbitrary impairment by state action has been judicially recognized as a right secured by the Constitution when such impairment resulted from dilution by a false tally, or by a refusal to count votes from arbitrarily selected precincts, or by a stuffing of the ballot box.

- *What is the complaint of the voters? How do they argue they are not represented in the state legislature?*

The very essence of civil liberty certainly consists in the right of every individual to claim the protection of the laws, whenever he receives an injury.

IV
Justiciability

In holding that the subject matter of this suit was not justiciable, the District Court relied on *Colegrove v. Green*, and subsequent per curiam cases. The court stated:
"From a review of these decisions, there can be no doubt that the federal rule . . . is that the federal courts . . . will not intervene in cases of this type to compel legislative reapportionment."
We understand the District Court to have read the cited cases as compelling the conclusion that, since the appellants sought to have a legislative apportionment held unconstitutional, their suit presented a "political question," and was therefore nonjusticiable. We hold that this challenge to an

apportionment presents no nonjusticiable "political question." The cited cases do not hold the contrary.

- *The Court states that the question within this case about how many people a representative represented is not a political question. Do you agree? Why or why not?*

Of course, the mere fact that the suit seeks protection of a political right does not mean it presents a political question. Such an objection "is little more than a play upon words." Rather, it is argued that apportionment cases, whatever the actual wording of the complaint, can involve no federal constitutional right except one resting on the guaranty of a republican form of government, and that complaints based on that clause have been held to present political questions which are nonjusticiable.

We hold that the claim pleaded here neither rests upon nor implicates the Guaranty Clause, and that its justiciability is therefore not foreclosed by our decisions of cases involving that clause. The District Court misinterpreted *Colegrove v. Green* and other decisions of this Court on which it relied. Appellants' claim that they are being denied equal protection is justiciable, and if discrimination is sufficiently shown, the right to relief under the Equal Protection Clause is not diminished by the fact that the discrimination relates to political rights. Our discussion, even at the price of extending this opinion, requires review of a number of political question cases, in order to expose the attributes of the doctrine—attributes which, in various settings, diverge, combine, appear, and disappear in seeming disorderliness. That review reveals that, in the Guaranty Clause cases and in the other "political question" cases, it is the relationship between the judiciary and the coordinate branches of the Federal Government, and not the federal judiciary's relationship to the States, which gives rise to the "political question." We have said that, in determining whether a question falls within [the political question] category, the appropriateness under our system of government of attributing finality to the action of the political departments and also the lack of satisfactory criteria for a judicial determination are dominant considerations.

- *The Court is now discussing when something is or is not a "political question." If it is a political question, it should be controlled by a different branch of government (the executive or legislative). If it is not a political question, the Court can review the fairness and constitutionality of the issue. They provide several examples below—which side seems to be the most reasonable one to control in this situation?*

The nonjusticiability of a political question is primarily a function of the separation of powers. Deciding whether a matter has in any measure been committed by the Constitution to another branch of government, or whether the action of that branch exceeds whatever authority has been committed, is itself a delicate exercise in constitutional interpretation, and is a responsibility of this Court as ultimate interpreter of the Constitution. To demonstrate this requires no less than to analyze representative cases and to infer from them the analytical threads that make up the political question doctrine. We shall then show that none of those threads catches this case.

Foreign relations: there are sweeping statements to the effect that all questions touching foreign relations are political questions. Yet it is error to suppose that every case or controversy which touches foreign relations lies beyond judicial cognizance. For example, though a court will not ordinarily inquire whether a treaty has been terminated, since on that question, "governmental action . . . must be regarded as of controlling importance," if there has been no conclusive "governmental action," then a court can construe a treaty, and may find it provides the answer. Though a court will not undertake to construe a treaty in a manner inconsistent with a subsequent federal statute, no similar hesitancy obtains if the asserted clash is with state law.

Dates of duration of hostilities: though it has been stated broadly that "the power which declared the necessity is the power to declare its cessation, and what the cessation requires," here too analysis reveals isolable reasons for the presence of political questions, underlying this Court's refusal to review the political departments' determination of when or whether a war has ended. Dominant is the need for finality in the political determination, for emergency's nature demands "[a] prompt and unhesitating obedience." Moreover, the cessation of hostilities does not necessarily end the war power. It was stated that the war power includes the power "to remedy the evils which have arisen from its rise and progress," and continues during that emergency. But deference rests on reason, not habit. The question in a particular case may not seriously implicate considerations of finality—*e.g.,* a public program of importance (rent control), yet not central to the emergency effort. Further, clearly definable criteria for decision may be available. In such case, the political question barrier falls away:

Validity of enactments: In *Coleman v. Miller*, this Court held that the questions of how long a proposed amendment to the Federal Constitution remained open to ratification, and what effect a prior rejection had on a subsequent ratification, were committed to congressional resolution and involved criteria of decision that necessarily escaped the judicial grasp. Similar considerations apply to the enacting process: "[t]he respect due to coequal and independent departments," and the need for finality and certainty about the status of a statute contribute to judicial reluctance to inquire whether, as passed, it complied with all requisite formalities. But it is not true that courts will never delve into a legislature's records upon such a quest: if the enrolled statute lacks an effective date, a court will not hesitate to seek it in the legislative journals in order to preserve the enactment. The political question doctrine, a tool for maintenance of governmental order, will not be so applied as to promote only disorder.

The status of Indian tribes: this Court's deference to the political departments in determining whether Indians are recognized as a tribe, while it reflects familiar attributes of political questions, also has a unique element in that the relation of the Indians to the United States is marked by peculiar and cardinal distinctions which exist nowhere else. . . . [The Indians are] domestic dependent nations . . . in a state of pupilage. Their relation to the United States resembles that of a ward to his guardian. Yet here, too, there is no blanket rule. While "It is for [Congress] . . . and not for the courts, to determine when the true interests of the Indian require his release from [the] condition of tutelage," . . . it is not meant by this that Congress may bring a community or body of people within the range of this power by arbitrarily calling them an Indian tribe. . . . Able to discern what is "distinctly Indian," the courts will strike down any heedless extension of that label. They will not stand impotent before an obvious instance of a manifestly unauthorized exercise of power.

It is apparent that several formulations which vary slightly according to the settings in which the questions arise may describe a political question, although each has one or more elements which identify it as essentially a function of the separation of powers. Prominent on the surface of any case held to involve a political question is found a textually demonstrable constitutional commitment of the issue to a coordinate political department; or a lack of judicially discoverable and manageable standards for resolving it; or the impossibility of deciding without an initial policy determination of a kind clearly for nonjudicial discretion; or the impossibility of a court's undertaking independent resolution without expressing lack of the respect due coordinate branches of government; or an unusual need for unquestioning adherence to a political decision already made; or the potentiality of embarrassment from multifarious pronouncements by various departments on one question.

Unless one of these formulations is inextricable from the case at bar, there should be no dismissal for nonjusticiability on the ground of a political question's presence. The doctrine of which we treat is one of "political questions," not one of "political cases." The courts cannot reject as "no law suit" a *bona fide* controversy as to whether some action denominated "political" exceeds constitutional authority. The cases we have reviewed show the necessity for discriminating inquiry into the precise facts and posture of the particular case, and the impossibility of resolution by any semantic cataloguing.

But it is argued that this case shares the characteristics of decisions that constitute a category not yet considered, cases concerning the Constitution's guaranty, in Article IV, § 4, of a republican form of government. A conclusion as to whether the case at bar does present a political question cannot be confidently reached until we have considered those cases with special care. We shall discover that Guaranty Clause claims involve those elements which define a "political question," and, for that reason and no other, they are nonjusticiable. In particular, we shall discover that the nonjusticiability of such claims has nothing to do with their touching upon matters of state governmental organization.

- *The Court introduces the Guaranty Clause from Article 4 of the Constitution, which states, "The United States shall guarantee to every State in this Union a Republican Form of Government." If the Court attempts to force Tennessee to change how they allot voting districts, is that ensuring or deterring the guarantee of a republican form of government?*

Under this article of the Constitution, it rests with Congress to decide what government is the established one in a state. For, as the United States guarantee to each state a republican government, Congress must necessarily decide what government is established in the state before it can determine whether it is republican or not. And when the senators and representatives of a state are admitted into the councils of the Union, the authority of the government under which they are appointed, as well as its republican character, is recognized by the proper constitutional authority. And its decision is binding on every other department of the government, and could not be questioned in a judicial tribunal. It is true that the contest in this case did not last long enough to bring the matter to this issue, and . . . Congress was not called upon to decide the controversy. Yet the right to decide is placed there, and not in the courts.

The Court has since refused to resort to the Guaranty Clause—which alone had been invoked for the purpose as the source of a constitutional standard for invalidating state action.

We come, finally, to the ultimate inquiry whether our precedents as to what constitutes a nonjusticiable "political question" bring the case before us under the umbrella of that doctrine. A natural beginning is to note whether any of the common characteristics which we have been able to identify and label descriptively are present. We find none: the question here is the consistency of state action with the Federal Constitution. We have no question decided, or to be decided, by a political branch of government coequal with this Court. Nor do we risk embarrassment of our government abroad, or grave disturbance at home if we take issue with Tennessee as to the constitutionality of her action here challenged. Nor need the appellants, in order to succeed in this action, ask the Court to enter upon policy determinations for which judicially manageable standards are lacking. Judicial standards under the Equal Protection Clause are well developed and familiar, and it has been open to courts since the enactment of the Fourteenth Amendment to determine, if, on the particular facts, they must, that a discrimination reflects no policy, but simply arbitrary and capricious action.

This case does, in one sense, involve the allocation of political power within a State, and the appellants might conceivably have added a claim under the Guaranty Clause. Of course, as we have seen, any reliance on that clause would be futile. But because any reliance on the Guaranty Clause could not have succeeded, it does not follow that appellants may not be heard on the equal protection claim which, in fact, they tender.

- *The Court mentions that it is not necessary to consult the Guaranty Clause of the Constitution to consider the question of whether the voters are equally represented in this case. The question can still be raised using the Fourteenth Amendment's Equal Protection Clause. Essentially it is noting that the equal protection claim alone would make this a question for the Court to consider. Do you agree?*

We conclude, then, that the nonjusticiability of claims resting on the Guaranty Clause, which arises from their embodiment of questions that were thought "political," can have no bearing upon the justiciability of the equal protection claim presented in this case. Since, as has been established, the equal protection claim tendered in this case does not require decision of any political question, and since the presence of a matter affecting state government does not render the case nonjusticiable, it seems appropriate to examine again the reasoning by which the District Court reached its conclusion that the case was nonjusticiable.

We conclude that the complaint's allegations of a denial of equal protection present a justiciable constitutional cause of action upon which appellants are entitled to a trial and a decision. The right asserted is within the reach of judicial protection under the Fourteenth Amendment.

The judgment of the District Court is reversed, and the cause is remanded for further proceedings consistent with this opinion.

Reversed and remanded.

Connecting, Arguing, and Analyzing the Case

1. *Baker v. Carr* is a demonstration of the Court determining what is outside its reach and what is within its reach. Are there issues the Court has considered that you would argue are so political in nature that the Court should have never heard the case? Why or why not?
2. The Court heard a case soon after the *Baker* case when it took on *Reynolds v. Sims* in 1964, where it required that state legislative bod-

ies be made up of equal representation. This ensured the principle of "one person, one vote" was in place, meaning that voting districts should receive equal representation based on the number of voters within the district boundaries—at least on the local level. Does the Constitution require that each vote count equally? Why or why not?
3. Recent U.S. Supreme Court cases have dealt with the issue of "gerrymandering," or drawing district political lines in order to favor one party or another. See a visual representation of gerrymandering from the *Washington Post* article "This is the Best Explanation of Gerrymandering You Will Ever See" by Christopher Ingraham here: https://www.washingtonpost.com/news/wonk/wp/2015/03/01/this-is-the-best-explanation-of-gerrymandering-you-will-ever-see/?noredirect=on&utm_term=.06d9a3dd042b. Is drawing lines in order to boost one party's voting numbers a violation of the Equal Protection Clause based on what we know from *Baker*? Why or why not?
4. The U.S. Supreme Court agreed to hear two cases related to "gerrymandering" during the 2018–2019 session. One of those cases, *Rucho v. Common Cause*, challenges a redrawing of North Carolina's voting districts that, the appellants argue, dilutes the strengths of the voters based on their political party, leading to favoring one party over the other. Does this violate the Fourteenth Amendment? Why or why not?

Chapter Six

Engel v. Vitale

The Establishment Clause of the First Amendment of the U.S. Constitution states: "*Congress shall make no law respecting an establishment of religion, or prohibiting the free exercise thereof; or abridging the freedom of speech, or of the press; or the right of the people peaceably to assemble, and to petition the government for a redress of grievances*" (emphasis added).

The Establishment Clause forbids the government from establishing national religion, but how far did that reach? Consideration of the Establishment Clause didn't happen until 1947 when the Court decided *Everson v. Board of Education*. The Court ruled that reimbursing parents for the cost of busing their children to parochial school did not violate the Establishment Clause. As the Court notes, James Madison "eloquently argued that a true religion did not need the support of law; that no person, either believer or nonbeliever, should be taxed to support a religious institution of any kind; that the best interest of a society required that the minds of men always be wholly free, and that cruel persecutions were the inevitable result of government-established religions" (*Everson v. Board of Education*, 330 U.S. 1 [1947].)

Different facts reached a different result a year later in *McCollum v. Board of Education* (1948) when the Court said that providing optional religious instruction in public school did violate the Establishment Clause, though allowing students out of school to receive religious instruction off school grounds was upheld in the 1952 decision *Zorach v. Clauson*. These cases set the backdrop for the school prayer case *Engel v. Vitale* in 1962.

Legal Issue

Does a school-sponsored, nondenominational prayer in a public school violate the Establishment Clause of the First Amendment?

Vocabulary

Recitation: repeating aloud
Amicus curiae: "one (such as a professional person or organization) that is not a party to a particular litigation but that is permitted by the court to advise it in respect to some matter of law that directly affects the case in question" (Merriam-Webster)
Nondenominational: not restricted to a certain religion or church
Coercive: an act that is compelled
Persecution: "to cause to suffer because of a belief" (Merriam-Webster)
Doctrine: the set of beliefs belonging to a religion
Invoke: "to put into effect" (Merriam-Webster)

Parties in the Case

Petitioner: Steven Engel, a parent of a pupil in the Union Free School District No. 9 and nine other parents of students
Respondent: Board of Education of Union Free School District No. 9, New Hyde Park, New York (William Vitale was the president of the school board)
Edited version of case in the original language with distractors removed

ENGEL V. VITALE, 370 U.S. 421 (1962)

MR. JUSTICE BLACK delivered the opinion of the Court.

The respondent Board of Education of Union Free School District No. 9, New Hyde Park, New York, acting in its official capacity under state law, directed the School District's principal to cause the following prayer to be said aloud by each class in the presence of a teacher at the beginning of each school day:

"Almighty God, we acknowledge our dependence upon Thee, and we beg Thy blessings upon us, our parents, our teachers and our Country."

- *Read the prayer and discuss whether the government is promoting one religion over another. What details support this? Is the prayer truly non-denominational? What makes it different from something like the Pledge of Allegiance, with its reference to "under God"?*

This daily procedure was adopted on the recommendation of the State Board of Regents, a governmental agency created by the State Constitution to which the New York Legislature has granted broad supervisory, executive, and legislative powers over the State's public school system. These state officials composed the prayer which they recommended and published as a

part of their "Statement on Moral and Spiritual Training in the Schools," saying:
"We believe that this Statement will be subscribed to by all men and women of good will, and we call upon all of them to aid in giving life to our program."

Shortly after the practice of reciting the Regents' prayer was adopted by the School District, the parents of ten pupils brought this action in a New York State Court insisting that use of this official prayer in the public schools was contrary to the beliefs, religions, or religious practices of both themselves and their children. Among other things, these parents challenged the constitutionality of both the state law authorizing the School District to direct the use of prayer in public schools and the School District's regulation ordering the recitation of this particular prayer on the ground that these actions of official governmental agencies violate that part of the First Amendment of the Federal Constitution which commands that "Congress shall make no law respecting an establishment of religion"—a command which was "made applicable to the State of New York by the Fourteenth Amendment of the said Constitution."

- *Who is bringing the action, and what are they challenging?*

The New York Court of Appeals, over the dissents of Judges Dye and Fuld, sustained an order of the lower state courts which had upheld the power of New York to use the Regents' prayer as a part of the daily procedures of its public schools so long as the schools did not compel any pupil to join in the prayer over his or his parents' objection.

- *Describe the decision of the lower court.*

We granted certiorari to review this important decision involving rights protected by the First and Fourteenth Amendments.

We think that, by using its public school system to encourage recitation of the Regents' prayer, the State of New York has adopted a practice wholly inconsistent with the Establishment Clause. There can, of course, be no doubt that New York's program of daily classroom invocation of God's blessings as prescribed in the Regents' prayer is a religious activity. It is a solemn avowal of divine faith and supplication for the blessings of the Almighty. The nature of such a prayer has always been religious, none of the respondents has denied this:

> The Board of Regents as *amicus curiae*, the respondents, and intervenors all concede the religious nature of prayer, but seek to distinguish this prayer because it is based on our spiritual heritage. . . .

The petitioners contend, among other things, that the state laws requiring or permitting use of the Regents' prayer must be struck down as a violation of the Establishment Clause because that prayer was composed by governmental officials as a part of a governmental program to further religious beliefs. For this reason, petitioners argue, the state's use of the Regents' prayer in its public school system breaches the constitutional wall of separation between church and state.

- *What differences exist between the two sides' arguments?*

We agree with that contention, since we think that the constitutional prohibition against laws respecting an establishment of religion must at least mean that, in this country, it is no part of the business of government to compose official prayers for any group of the American people to recite as a part of a religious program carried on by government.

- *Do you agree that the prayer in public school violates the Establishment Clause?*

It is a matter of history that this very practice of establishing governmentally composed prayers for religious services was one of the reasons which caused many of our early colonists to leave England and seek religious freedom in America.

There can be no doubt that New York's state prayer program officially establishes the religious beliefs embodied in the Regents' prayer. The respondents' argument to the contrary, which is largely based upon the contention that the Regents' prayer is "nondenominational" and the fact that the program, as modified and approved by state courts, does not require all pupils to recite the prayer, but permits those who wish to do so to remain silent or be excused from the room, ignores the essential nature of the program's constitutional defects. Neither the fact that the prayer may be denominationally neutral nor the fact that its observance on the part of the students is voluntary can serve to free it from the limitations of the Establishment Clause, as it might from the Free Exercise Clause, of the First Amendment, both of which are operative against the States by virtue of the Fourteenth Amendment. Although these two clauses may, in certain instances, overlap, they forbid two quite different kinds of governmental encroachment upon religious freedom. The Establishment Clause, unlike the Free Exercise Clause, does not depend upon any showing of direct governmental compulsion and is violated by the enactment of laws which establish an official religion whether those laws operate directly to coerce nonobserving individuals or not. This is not to say, of course, that laws officially prescribing a particular form of religious worship do not involve coercion of such individuals. When the power, prestige and financial support of government is placed behind a particular religious belief, the indirect coercive pressure upon religious minorities to conform to the prevailing officially approved religion is plain.

But the purposes underlying the Establishment Clause go much further than that. Its first and most immediate purpose rested on the belief that a union of government and religion tends to destroy government and to degrade religion. The history of governmentally established religion, both in England and in this country, showed that whenever government had allied itself with one particular form of religion, the inevitable result had been that it had incurred the hatred, disrespect and even contempt of those who held contrary beliefs. That same history showed that many people had lost their respect for any religion that had relied upon the support of government to spread its faith. The Establishment Clause thus stands as an expression of principle on the part of the Founders of our Constitution that religion is too personal, too sacred, too holy, to permit its "unhallowed perversion" by a civil magistrate.

- *How does the Court contrast the Establishment Clause and the Free Exercise Clause?*

Another purpose of the Establishment Clause rested upon an awareness of the historical fact that governmentally established religions and religious persecutions go hand in hand. The Founders knew that, only a few years after the Book of Common Prayer became the only accepted form of religious services in the established Church of England, an Act of Uniformity was passed to compel all Englishmen to attend those services and to make it a criminal offense to conduct or attend religious gatherings of any other kind— a law which was consistently flouted by dissenting religious groups in England and which contributed to widespread persecutions of people like John Bunyan who persisted in holding "unlawful [religious] meetings . . . to the great disturbance and distraction of the good subjects of this kingdom. . . ." And they knew that similar persecutions had received the sanction of law in several of the colonies in this country soon after the establishment of official religions in those colonies. It was in large part to get completely away from this sort of systematic religious persecution that the Founders brought into being our Nation, our Constitution, and our Bill of Rights, with its prohibition against any governmental establishment of religion. The New York laws officially prescribing the Regents' prayer are inconsistent both with the purposes of the Establishment Clause and with the Establishment Clause itself.

- *Why is religion a highly personal decision, so much so that the authors of the Constitution mentioned it twice—the freedom to choose your own* religion but also the freedom from the government establishing a religion that one must practice?

It is true that New York's establishment of its Regents' prayer as an officially approved religious doctrine of that State does not amount to a total establishment of one particular religious sect to the exclusion of all others—that, indeed, the governmental endorsement of that prayer seems relatively insignificant when compared to the governmental encroachments upon religion which were commonplace 200 years ago. To those who may subscribe to the view that, because the Regents' official prayer is so brief and general there can be no danger to religious freedom in its governmental establishment, however, it may be appropriate to say in the words of James Madison, the author of the First Amendment:

> [I]t is proper to take alarm at the first experiment on our liberties. . . . Who does not see that the same authority which can establish Christianity, in exclusion of all other Religions, may establish with the same ease any particular sect of Christians, in exclusion of all other Sects? That the same authority which can force a citizen to contribute three pence only of his property for the support of any one establishment may force him to conform to any other establishment in all cases whatsoever?

The judgment of the Court of Appeals of New York is reversed, and the cause remanded for further proceedings not inconsistent with this opinion.

Reversed and remanded.

MR. JUSTICE FRANKFURTER took no part in the decision of this case.

MR. JUSTICE WHITE took no part in the consideration or decision of this case.

MR. JUSTICE DOUGLAS, concurring.

It is customary in deciding a constitutional question to treat it in its narrowest form. Yet at times the setting of the question gives it a form and content which no abstract treatment could give. The point for decision is whether the Government can constitutionally finance a religious exercise. Our system at the federal and state levels is presently honeycombed with such financing. Nevertheless, I think it is an unconstitutional undertaking whatever form it takes.

In New York, the teacher who leads in prayer is on the public payroll, and the time she takes seems minuscule as compared with the salaries appropriated by state legislatures and Congress for chaplains to conduct prayers in the legislative halls. Only a bare fraction of the teacher's time is given to reciting this short twenty-two word prayer, about the same amount of time that our Crier spends announcing the opening of our sessions and offering a prayer for this Court. Yet, for me, the principle is the same, no matter how briefly the prayer is said, for, in each of the instances given, the person praying is a public official on the public payroll, performing a religious exercise in a governmental institution.

What New York does with this prayer is a break with that tradition. I therefore join the Court in reversing the judgment below.

- *How is Justice Douglas's concurring opinion narrower than the majority opinion?*

MR. JUSTICE STEWART, dissenting.

A local school board in New York has provided that those pupils who wish to do so may join in a brief prayer at the beginning of each school day, acknowledging their dependence upon God and asking His blessing upon them and upon their parents, their teachers, and their country. The Court today decides that, in permitting this brief nondenominational prayer, the school board has violated the Constitution of the United States. I think this decision is wrong.

The Court does not hold, nor could it, that New York has interfered with the free exercise of anybody's religion. For the state courts have made clear that those who object to reciting the prayer must be entirely free of any compulsion to do so, including any "embarrassments and pressures." *Cf. West Virginia State Board of Education v. Barnette.* But the Court says that, in permitting school children to say this simple prayer, the New York authorities have established "an official religion."

With all respect, I think the Court has misapplied a great constitutional principle. I cannot see how an "official religion" is established by letting those who want to say a prayer say it. On the contrary, I think that to deny the wish of these school children to join in reciting this prayer is to deny them the opportunity of sharing in the spiritual heritage of our Nation.

At the opening of each day's Session of this Court we stand, while one of our officials invokes the protection of God. Since the days of John Marshall, our Crier has said, "God save the United States and this Honorable Court." Both the Senate and the House of Representatives open their daily Sessions with prayer. Each of our presidents, from George Washington to John F. Kennedy, has, upon assuming his office, asked the protection and help of God.

The Court today says that the state and federal governments are without constitutional power to prescribe any particular form of words to be recited by any group of the American people on any subject touching religion. One of the stanzas of "The Star-Spangled Banner," made our National Anthem by Act of Congress in 1931, contains these verses:

"Blest with victory and peace, may the heav'n rescued land"
"Praise the Pow'r that hath made and preserved us a nation,"
"Then conquer we must, when our cause it is just."

"And this be our motto 'In God is our Trust.'"

In 1954, Congress added a phrase to the Pledge of Allegiance to the Flag so that it now contains the words "one Nation *under* God, indivisible, with liberty and justice for all." In 1952, Congress enacted legislation calling upon the president each year to proclaim a National Day of Prayer. Since 1865, the words "IN GOD WE TRUST" have been impressed on our coins. Countless similar examples could be listed, but there is no need to belabor the obvious. It was all summed up by this Court just ten years ago in a single sentence: "We are a religious people whose institutions presuppose a Supreme Being." *Zorach v. Clauson.*

I do not believe that this Court, or the Congress, or the president has, by the actions and practices I have mentioned, established an "official religion" in violation of the Constitution. And I do not believe the State of New York has done so in this case. What each has done has been to recognize and to follow the deeply entrenched and highly cherished spiritual traditions of our Nation—traditions which come down to us from those who almost two hundred years ago avowed their "firm Reliance on the Protection of divine Providence" when they proclaimed the freedom and independence of this brave new world.

- *How is the dissent's interpretation of the establishment clause different than the majority opinion? What evidence does Justice Stewart use to support his opinion?*

I dissent.

Connecting, Arguing, and Analyzing the Case

1. In *Wallace v. Jaffree* (1985), the Court found an Alabama statute that mandated a moment of silence in schools for the purpose of "meditation or prayer" violated the establishment clause. Using the reasoning of *Engel v. Vitale* (1962) and *Wallace v. Jaffree* (1985), argue that a moment of silence with a secular purpose is constitutional.
2. Consider the case where a student leads her classmates in a prayer during the moment of silence. The principal forbids the student from praying vocally. Is this a violation of the student's freedom of expression?
3. Discuss how schools should balance students' freedom of expression with the Establishment Clause.
4. In *Santa Fe Independent School District v. Doe* (2000), the school allowed a student-led, student-prepared prayer before football games. One Mormon and one Catholic family challenged the practice as a

violation of the Establishment Clause of the First Amendment. The Court held that this practice did violate the Establishment Clause.

    a. Identify the constitutional clause that is common to both *Santa Fe Independent School District v. Doe* (2000) and *Engel v. Vitale* (1962).

    b. Based on the constitutional clause identified in part a, explain the facts of *Santa Fe Independent School District v. Doe* (2000) and *Engel v. Vitale* (1962).

    c. Describe actions that schools who disagree with the holding in *Santa Fe Independent School District v. Doe* (2000) could take in order to honor students' desire to pray.

Chapter Seven

Gideon v. Wainwright

The right to counsel found in the Sixth Amendment states that: "*In all criminal prosecutions, the accused shall enjoy the right to* a speedy and public trial, by an impartial jury of the state and district wherein the crime shall have been committed, which district shall have been previously ascertained by law, and to be informed of the nature and cause of the accusation; to be confronted with the witnesses against him; to have compulsory process for obtaining witnesses in his favor, and to have *the Assistance of Counsel for his defence*" (emphasis added).

By 1963, the Court had dealt with the Sixth Amendment right to counsel. The Court, in 1932, decided in *Powell v. Alabama* that the right extended to defendants charged with capital crimes. The Court limited the right in 1942 with its decision in *Betts v. Brady*. The Court held that there was no right to counsel in felony cases unless there were special circumstances. In *Gideon v. Wainwright*, the Court faced the question of whether to overturn *Betts v. Brady*.

As Robert F. Kennedy said, Gideon's letter changed history:

> If an obscure Florida convict named Clarence Earl Gideon had not sat down in prison with a pencil and paper to write a letter to the Supreme Court; and if the Supreme Court had not taken the trouble to look at the merits in that one crude petition among all the bundles of mail it must receive every day, the vast machinery of American law would have gone on functioning undisturbed. But Gideon did write that letter; the court did look into his case; he was re-tried with the help of competent defense counsel; found not guilty and released from prison after two years of punishment for a crime he did not commit. And the whole course of legal history has been changed.

Legal Issue

Does the Sixth Amendment right to counsel in felony cases extend to state court?

Vocabulary

Colloquy: "high-level, serious discussion" (Merriam-Webster)
Layman: a person who is not an expert in the law
Habeas corpus: "a writ for inquiring into the lawfulness of the restraint of a person who is imprisoned or detained in another's custody" (Merriam-Webster)
In forma pauperis: "as a poor person" (Merriam-Webster)
Precedent: "earlier laws or decisions that provide some example or rule to guide them in the case they're actually deciding" (Merriam-Webster)
Adversary: opposing interests

Parties in the Case

Petitioner: Clarence Earl Gideon
Respondent: Louie L. Wainwright, director, Division of Corrections
   Edited version of case in the original language with distractors removed.

GIDEON V. WAINWRIGHT, 372 U.S. 335 (1963)

MR. JUSTICE BLACK delivered the opinion of the Court.
   Petitioner was charged in a Florida state court with having broken and entered a poolroom with intent to commit a misdemeanor. This offense is a felony under Florida law. Appearing in court without funds and without a lawyer, petitioner asked the court to appoint counsel for him, whereupon the following colloquy took place:
   "The COURT: Mr. Gideon, I am sorry, but I cannot appoint Counsel to represent you in this case. Under the laws of the State of Florida, the only time the Court can appoint Counsel to represent a Defendant is when that person is charged with a capital offense. I am sorry, but I will have to deny your request to appoint Counsel to defend you in this case."
   "The DEFENDANT: The United States Supreme Court says I am entitled to be represented by Counsel."

- *Under the current law, when does a defendant have the right to counsel in a state court?*

Put to trial before a jury, Gideon conducted his defense about as well as could be expected from a layman. He made an opening statement to the jury, cross-examined the state's witnesses, presented witnesses in his own defense, declined to testify himself, and made a short argument "emphasizing his innocence to the charge contained in the Information filed in this case." The jury returned a verdict of guilty, and petitioner was sentenced to serve five years in the state prison. Later, petitioner filed in the Florida Supreme Court this habeas corpus petition attacking his conviction and sentence on the ground that the trial court's refusal to appoint counsel for him denied him rights "guaranteed by the Constitution and the Bill of Rights by the United States Government." Treating the petition for habeas corpus as properly before it, the State Supreme Court, "upon consideration thereof" but without an opinion, denied all relief. Since 1942, when *Betts v. Brady* was decided by a divided Court, the problem of a defendant's federal constitutional right to counsel in a state court has been a continuing source of controversy and litigation in both state and federal courts.

- *What was the holding in* Betts v. Brady?

To give this problem another review here, we granted certiorari. 370 U.S. 908. Since Gideon was proceeding *in forma pauperis*, we appointed counsel to represent him and requested both sides to discuss in their briefs and oral arguments the following: "Should this Court's holding in *Betts v. Brady* be reconsidered?"

- *What would be the state's interest in having a defendant secure the representation of a lawyer?*

I

The facts upon which Betts claimed that he had been unconstitutionally denied the right to have counsel appointed to assist him are strikingly like the facts upon which Gideon here bases his federal constitutional claim. Betts was indicted for robbery in a Maryland state court. On arraignment, he told the trial judge of his lack of funds to hire a lawyer and asked the court to appoint one for him. Betts was advised that it was not the practice in that county to appoint counsel for indigent defendants except in murder and rape cases. He then pleaded not guilty, had witnesses summoned, cross-examined the State's witnesses, examined his own, and chose not to testify himself. He was found guilty by the judge, sitting without a jury, and sentenced to eight years in prison. Like Gideon, Betts sought release by habeas corpus, alleging that he had been denied the right to assistance of counsel in violation of the Fourteenth Amendment. Betts was denied any relief, and, on review, this Court affirmed. It was held that a refusal to appoint counsel for an indigent defendant charged with a felony did not necessarily violate the Due Process

Clause of the Fourteenth Amendment, which, for reasons given, the Court deemed to be the only applicable federal constitutional provision. The Court said:

"Asserted denial [of due process] is to be tested by an appraisal of the totality of facts in a given case. That which may, in one setting, constitute a denial of fundamental fairness, shocking to the universal sense of justice, may, in other circumstances, and in the light of other considerations, fall short of such denial." Treating due process as "a concept less rigid and more fluid than those envisaged in other specific and particular provisions of the Bill of Rights," the Court held that refusal to appoint counsel under the particular facts and circumstances in the *Betts* case was not so "offensive to the common and fundamental ideas of fairness" as to amount to a denial of due process. Since the facts and circumstances of the two cases are so nearly indistinguishable, we think the *Betts v. Brady* holding, if left standing, would require us to reject Gideon's claim that the Constitution guarantees him the assistance of counsel.

Upon full reconsideration, we conclude that *Betts v. Brady* should be overruled.

- *Summarize the Court's reasoning in* Betts *that not appointing counsel for indigent clients in felony cases did not violate the Due Process Clause. What is the importance of the Fourteenth Amendment?*

II

The Sixth Amendment provides, "In all criminal prosecutions, the accused shall enjoy the right . . . to have the Assistance of Counsel for his defence." We have construed this to mean that, in federal courts, counsel must be provided for defendants unable to employ counsel unless the right is competently and intelligently waived. Betts argued that this right is extended to indigent defendants in state courts by the Fourteenth Amendment. In response, the Court stated that, while the Sixth Amendment laid down "no rule for the conduct of the States, the question recurs whether the constraint laid by the Amendment upon the national courts expresses a rule so fundamental and essential to a fair trial, and so, to due process of law, that it is made obligatory upon the States by the Fourteenth Amendment."

In order to decide whether the Sixth Amendment's guarantee of counsel is of this fundamental nature, the Court in *Betts* set out and considered "[r]elevant data on the subject . . . afforded by constitutional and statutory provisions subsisting in the colonies and the States prior to the inclusion of the Bill of Rights in the national Constitution, and in the constitutional, legislative, and judicial history of the States to the present date." On the basis of this historical data, the Court concluded that "appointment of counsel is not a fundamental right, essential to a fair trial." It was for this reason the *Betts* Court refused to accept the contention that the Sixth Amendment's guarantee of counsel for indigent federal defendants was extended to or, in the words of that Court, "made obligatory upon, the States by the Fourteenth Amendment." Plainly, had the Court concluded that appointment of counsel for an indigent criminal defendant was "a fundamental right, essential to a fair trial," it would have held that the Fourteenth Amendment requires appointment of counsel in a state court, just as the Sixth Amendment requires in a federal court.

We think the Court in *Betts* had ample precedent for acknowledging that those guarantees of the Bill of Rights which are fundamental safeguards of liberty immune from federal abridgment are equally protected against state invasion by the Due Process Clause of the Fourteenth Amendment.

- *What makes a guarantee of the Bill of Rights a "fundamental safeguard of liberty"?*

We accept *Betts v. Brady*'s assumption, based as it was on our prior cases, that a provision of the Bill of Rights which is "fundamental and essential to a fair trial" is made obligatory upon the states by the Fourteenth Amendment. We think the Court in *Betts* was wrong, however, in concluding that the Sixth Amendment's guarantee of counsel is not one of these fundamental rights. Ten years before *Betts v. Brady*, this Court, after full consideration of all the historical data examined in *Betts*, had unequivocally declared that "the right to the aid of counsel is of this fundamental character" *Powell v. Alabama.* While the Court, at the close of its *Powell* opinion, did, by its language, as this Court frequently does, limit its holding to the particular facts and circumstances of that case, its conclusions about the fundamental nature of the right to counsel are unmistakable. Several years later, in 1936, the Court reemphasized what it had said about the fundamental nature of the right to counsel in this language:

"We concluded that certain fundamental rights, safeguarded by the first eight amendments against federal action, were also safeguarded against state action by the due process of law clause of the Fourteenth Amendment, and among them the fundamental right of the accused to the aid of counsel in a criminal prosecution." *Grosjean v. American Press Co.*

The fact is that, in deciding as it did—that "appointment of counsel is not a fundamental right, essential to a fair trial"—the Court in *Betts v. Brady* made an abrupt break with its own well considered precedents. In returning to these old precedents, sounder, we believe, than the new, we but restore constitutional principles established to achieve a fair system of justice. Not only these precedents, but also reason and reflection, require us to recognize that, in our adversary system of criminal justice, any person haled into court, who is too poor to hire a lawyer, cannot be assured a fair trial unless counsel is provided for him. This seems to us to be an obvious truth. Governments, both state and federal, quite properly spend vast sums of money to establish machinery to try defendants accused of crime. Lawyers to prosecute are everywhere deemed essential to protect the public's interest in an orderly society.

Similarly, there are few defendants charged with crime, few indeed, who fail to hire the best lawyers they can get to prepare and present their defenses. That government hires lawyers to prosecute and defendants who have the money hire lawyers to defend are the strongest indications of the widespread belief that lawyers in criminal courts are necessities, not luxuries. The right of one charged with crime to counsel may not be deemed fundamental and essential to fair trials in some countries, but it is in ours. From the very beginning, our state and national constitutions and laws have laid great emphasis on procedural and substantive safeguards designed to assure fair trials before impartial tribunals in which every defendant stands equal before the law. This noble ideal cannot be realized if the poor man charged with crime has to face his accusers without a lawyer to assist him. A defendant's need for a lawyer is nowhere better stated than in the moving words of Mr. Justice Sutherland in *Powell v. Alabama*:

> The right to be heard would be, in many cases, of little avail if it did not comprehend the right to be heard by counsel. Even the intelligent and educated layman has small and sometimes no skill in the science of law. If charged with crime, he is incapable, generally, of determining for himself whether the indictment is good or bad. He is unfamiliar with the rules of evidence. Left without the aid of counsel, he may be put on trial without a proper charge, and convicted upon incompetent evidence, or evidence irrelevant to the issue or otherwise inadmissible. He lacks both the skill and knowledge adequately to prepare his defense, even though he have a perfect one. He requires the guiding hand of counsel at every step in the proceedings against him. Without it, though he be not guilty, he faces the danger of conviction because he does not know how to establish his innocence.

- *Describe the Court's reasoning in* Powell.

The Court in *Betts v. Brady* departed from the sound wisdom upon which the Court's holding in *Powell v. Alabama* rested. Florida, supported by two other States, has asked that *Betts v. Brady* be left intact. Twenty-two States, as friends of the Court, argue that *Betts* was "an anachronism when handed down," and that it should now be overruled. We agree.

- *What is the Court's reasoning in overturning* Betts?

The judgment is reversed, and the cause is remanded to the Supreme Court of Florida for further action not inconsistent with this opinion.
Reversed.

Connecting, Arguing, and Analyzing the Case

1. In Gideon's subsequent trial, he was found not guilty. Compare and contrast the differences between the two trials.
2. Clarence Gideon handwrote his petition to the U.S. Supreme Court from prison. The original petition can be found on the National Archives website. Different organizations filed amicus curiae briefs to the Supreme Court about this case. An amicus curiae brief is a written submission to the Court by a party not directly involved in the case but who believes there is important information that the Court should hear from them about the case to help the Court make its decision. Write your own amicus brief where you give your reasoning to support either the petitioner or respondent's point of view from your own experience.
3. Consider the case of Jon Argersinger, an indigent person, charged with a concealed weapon, a misdemeanor. In the state of Florida, the maximum sentence was a penalty of six months and $1,000 fine. Argersinger did not have representation of counsel. Does the Sixth and Fourteenth Amendments guarantee the right to counsel in cases of all misdemeanors? The Court extended the right to counsel found in *Gideon v. Wainwright* to misdemeanors that carried the possibility of a jail sentence. Explain how the interests that the Court was protecting in *Gideon v. Wainwright* (1963) are relevant in *Argersinger v. Hamlin* (1972).
4. David Washington pleaded guilty to murder and was sentenced to death. Washington sought habeas corpus claiming that his Sixth Amendment right to counsel was violated because his counsel was ineffective at the sentencing hearing. The Court in *Strickland v. Washington* (1984) held that a defendant's Sixth Amendment right to an attorney is violated if the counsel's performance falls below an "objective standard of reasonableness" and the result of the trial would have been different but for the attorney's below standard performance.

   a. Identify the constitutional clause that is common to both *Gideon v. Wainwright* (1963) and *Strickland v. Washington* (1984).
   b. Using the reasoning of *Gideon v. Wainwright* (1963), write a dissent for *Strickland v. Washington* (1984).

Chapter Eight

Tinker v. Des Moines Independent Community School District

The Freedom of Speech Clause found in the First Amendment of the U.S. Constitution states that *"Congress shall make no law* respecting an establishment of religion, or prohibiting the free exercise thereof; or *abridging the freedom of speech*, or of the press; or the right of the people peaceably to assemble, and to petition the government for a redress of grievances" (emphasis added).

As the ancient Greeks recognized, freedom of speech was the pinnacle ideal of a democracy. In the United States, the First Amendment articulates our freedom of speech, but this right is not absolute. The Supreme Court has decided many cases deciding what qualifies as "speech" and the limits that can be placed on this individual liberty.

Until 1943, a student's freedom of expression in a school was virtually nonexistent. In 1943, the Court decided *West Virginia State Board of Education v. Barnette*. The Court determined that it was a violation of the students' First Amendment right if they were required to stand, salute the flag, and recite the Pledge of Allegiance.

But it was in 1969, when the Court decided *Tinker v. Des Moines Independent Community School District*, that the idea of students having First Amendment rights that they didn't "shed at the schoolhouse gates" exploded.

Legal Issue

Did the public school violate the students' First Amendment freedom of expression when the school punished the students for wearing the black armbands?

Vocabulary

Compelled: forced to do something
Nascent: "coming or having recently come in existence" (Merriam-Webster)
Undifferentiated: not distinguished from other characteristics
Regimentation: "to subject to order or uniformity" (Merriam-Webster)
Prohibition: "prevent from doing something" (Merriam-Webster)
Enclaves: a unit within a larger unit

Parties in the Case

Petitioner: John Tinker, Mary Beth Tinker, and Christopher Eckhart; three public school students
Respondent: Des Moines Independent Community School District
 Edited version of case in the original language with distractors removed.

TINKER V. DES MOINES INDEPENDENT COMMUNITY SCHOOL DISTRICT, 393 U.S. 503 (1969)

JUSTICE ABE FORTAS delivered the opinion of the Court.

Petitioner John F. Tinker, 15 years old, and petitioner Christopher Eckhardt, 16 years old, attended high schools in Des Moines, Iowa. Petitioner Mary Beth Tinker, John's sister, was a 13-year-old student in junior high school.

In December 1965, a group of adults and students in Des Moines held a meeting at the Eckhardt home. The group determined to publicize their objections to the hostilities in Vietnam and their support for a truce by wearing black armbands during the holiday season and by fasting on December 16 and New Year's Eve. Petitioners and their parents had previously engaged in similar activities, and they decided to participate in the programs.

The principals of the Des Moines schools became aware of the plan to wear armbands.

On December 14, 1965, they met and adopted a policy that any student wearing an armband to school would be asked to remove it, and if he refused he would be suspended until he returned without the armband. Petitioners were aware of the regulation that the school authorities adopted.

On December 16, Mary Beth and Christopher wore black armbands to their schools. John Tinker wore his armband the next day. They were all sent home and suspended from school until they would come back without their armbands. They did not return to school until after the planned period for wearing armbands had expired—that is, until after New Year's Day.

- *Describe the facts of the case (include the who, what, why, where, and when).*

I

First Amendment rights, applied in light of the special characteristics of the school environment, are available to teachers and students. It can hardly be argued that either students or teachers shed their constitutional rights to freedom of speech or expression at the schoolhouse gate. This has been the unmistakable holding of this Court for almost 50 years.

In *West Virginia v. Barnette*, this Court held that under the First Amendment, the student in public school may not be compelled to salute the flag.

On the other hand, the Court has repeatedly emphasized the need for affirming the comprehensive authority of the States and of school officials, consistent with fundamental constitutional safeguards, to prescribe and control conduct in the schools.

- *Compare and contrast the Court's previous rulings regarding the First Amendment rights in schools. What interests are to be considered in these cases?*

Our problem lies in the area where students in the exercise of First Amendment rights collide with the rules of the school authorities.

- *What criteria would you use to assess whether the students' First Amendment rights were violated?*

II

The school officials banned and sought to punish petitioners for a silent, passive expression of opinion, unaccompanied by any disorder or disturbance on the part of petitioners. There is here no evidence whatever of petitioners' interference, actual or nascent, with the schools' work or of collision with the rights of other students to be secure and to be let alone. Accordingly, this case does not concern speech or action that intrudes upon the work of the schools or the rights of other students.

Only a few of the 18,000 students in the school system wore the black armbands. Only five students were suspended for wearing them. There is no indication that the work of the schools or any class was disrupted. Outside the classrooms, a few students made hostile remarks to the children wearing armbands, but there were no threats or acts of violence on school premises.

- *List the factors that the Court is considering in this case.*

The District Court concluded that the action of the school authorities was reasonable because it was based upon their fear of a disturbance from the wearing of the armbands. But, in our system, undifferentiated fear or apprehension of disturbance is not enough to overcome the right to freedom of expression. Any departure from absolute regimentation may cause trouble. Any variation from the majority's opinion may inspire fear. Any word spoken, in class, in the lunchroom, or on the campus, that deviates from the views of another person may start an argument or cause a disturbance. But our Constitution says we must take this risk, and our history says that it is this sort of hazardous freedom—this kind of openness—that is the basis of our national strength and of the independence and vigor of Americans who grow up and live in this relatively permissive, often disputatious, society.

- *Explain the reasoning of the district court when it decided that the school's punishment of the students was constitutional.*

In order for the State in the person of school officials to justify prohibition of a particular expression of opinion, it must be able to show that its action was caused by something more than a mere desire to avoid the discomfort and unpleasantness that always accompany an unpopular viewpoint. Certainly where there is no finding and no showing that engaging in the forbidden conduct would "materially and substantially interfere with the requirements of appropriate discipline in the operation of the school," the prohibition cannot be sustained.

- *What is the rule of law? What are examples that you think the court would consider "a substantial disruption"?*

In the present case, the District Court made no such finding, and our independent examination of the record fails to yield evidence that the school authorities had reason to anticipate that the wearing of the armbands would substantially interfere with the work of the school or impinge upon the rights of other students. Even an official memorandum prepared after the suspension that listed the reasons for the ban on wearing the armbands made no reference to the anticipation of such disruption.

On the contrary, the action of the school authorities appears to have been based upon an urgent wish to avoid the controversy which might result from the expression, even by the silent symbol of armbands, of opposition to this Nation's part in the conflagration in Vietnam. It is revealing, in this respect, that the meeting at which the school principals decided to issue the contested regulation was called in response to a student's statement to the journalism teacher in one of the schools that he wanted to write an article on Vietnam and have it published in the school paper.

- *What type of evidence would the school have had to present to justify the punishment of the students?*

It is also relevant that the school authorities did not purport to prohibit the wearing of all symbols of political or controversial significance. The record shows that students in some of the schools wore buttons relating to national political campaigns, and some even wore the Iron Cross, traditionally a symbol of Nazism. The order prohibiting the wearing of armbands did not extend to these. Instead, a particular symbol—black armbands worn to exhibit opposition to this Nation's involvement in Vietnam—was singled out for prohibition. Clearly, the prohibition of expression of one particular opinion, at least without evidence that it is necessary to avoid material and substantial interference with schoolwork or discipline, is not constitutionally permissible.

In our system, state-operated schools may not be enclaves of totalitarianism. School officials do not possess absolute authority over their students. Students in school as well as out of school are "persons" under our Constitution. They are possessed of fundamental rights which the state must respect, just as they themselves must respect their obligations to the state. In our system, students may not be regarded as closed-circuit recipients of only that which the state chooses to communicate. They may not be confined to the expression of those sentiments that are officially approved. In the absence of a specific showing of constitutionally valid reasons to regulate their speech, students are entitled to freedom of expression of their views. As Judge Gewin, speaking for the Fifth Circuit, said, school officials cannot suppress "expressions of feelings with which they do not wish to contend" (*Burnside v. Byars*).

- *Explain, in your own words, what the Court is saying. What seems to be important to the Court? What do the justices value?*

Under our Constitution, free speech is not a right that is given only to be so circumscribed that it exists in principle but not in fact. Freedom of expression would not truly exist if the right could be exercised only in an area that a benevolent government has provided as a safe haven for crackpots. The Constitution says that Congress (and the states) may not abridge the right to free speech. This provision means what it says. We properly read it to permit reasonable regulation of speech-connected activities in carefully restricted circumstances. But we do not confine the permissible exercise of First Amendment rights to a telephone booth or the four corners of a pamphlet, or to supervised and ordained discussion in a school classroom.

- *What is considered "speech"?*

If a regulation were adopted by school officials forbidding discussion of the Vietnam conflict, or the expression by any student of opposition to it anywhere on school property except as part of a prescribed classroom exercise, it would be obvious that the regulation would violate the constitutional rights of students, at least if it could not be justified by a showing that the students' activities would materially and substantially disrupt the work and discipline of the school. In the circumstances of the present case, the prohibition of the silent, passive "witness of the armbands," as one of the children called it, is no less offensive to the Constitution guarantees.

- *Predict the outcome if the record would have shown that other students were yelling at the students wearing the armbands in the hallway. Support your answer with evidence from the case.*

As we have discussed, the record does not demonstrate any facts which might reasonably have led school authorities to forecast substantial disruption of or material interference with school activities, and no disturbances or disorders on the school premises in fact occurred. These petitioners merely went about their ordained rounds in school. Their deviation consisted only in wearing on their sleeve a band of black cloth, not more than two inches wide. They wore it to exhibit their disapproval of the Vietnam hostilities and their advocacy of a truce, to make their views known, and, by their example, to influence others to adopt them. They neither interrupted school activities nor sought to intrude in the school affairs or the lives of others. They caused discussion outside of the classrooms, but no interference with work and no disorder. In the circumstances, our Constitution does not permit officials of the State to deny their form of expression.

Reversed and remanded.

Connecting, Arguing, and Analyzing the Case

1. Discuss how schools should balance interests of the school against the personal rights and freedoms of the students. Our society places a high priority on a citizen's First Amendment rights, especially political speech. Walkouts have been happening at schools in order for students to voice their opinions regarding gun violence. How does a school encourage student involvement in the democracy while minimizing the disruption to learning? How does a school respect the voices of all students?
2. You have decided that you want to organize a walkout in response to a recent school shooting (you can be on either side of the issue). Write a letter to your principal explaining and justifying your walkout. Use *Tinker* as your standard.

3. Consider the case where a student wears a t-shirt to school with the caption "International Terrorist" and a picture of George W. Bush's face. The principal makes the student turn the t-shirt inside out because she fears the t-shirt will cause a disruption. Does forbidding the student to wear the t-shirt violate his freedom of speech?
4. Matthew Fraser, a student at Bethel High School, gave a speech at an all-school assembly supporting his friend for an elected school position. The speech contained sexual innuendos such as "firm in his pants" and "climax." The school suspended Fraser and Fraser sued, claiming a violation of his First Amendment rights.

   In the ensuing case, *Bethel v. Fraser* (1986), the Supreme Court held in a 7–2 decision that no constitutional violation existed. The majority opinion stated that in this situation the school had a right to protect the younger students from inappropriate content.

   a. Identify the constitutional clause that is common to both *Bethel v. Fraser* (1986) and *Tinker v. Des Moines* (1969).
   b. Based on the constitutional clause identified in part A, explain why the facts of *Tinker v. Des Moines* (1969) led to a different holding in *Bethel v. Fraser* (1986).
   c. Describe an action that students who disagree with the holding in *Bethel v. Fraser* (1986) could take to limit its impact.

Chapter Nine

New York Times Co. v. United States

The First Amendment of the United States Constitution reads, "Congress shall make no law respecting an establishment of religion, or prohibiting the free exercise thereof; or abridging the freedom of speech, or of the press; or the right of the people peaceably to assemble, and to petition the Government for a redress of grievances." Notice the components of the nation that are protected under the First Amendment: freedom of religion, freedom of speech, and freedom of the press.

This case arose during the Vietnam War in the late 1960s and early 1970s, a time where the American public was growing disenchanted with a war that had gone on for over a decade. Daniel Ellsberg, a former military analyst and employee at a government research institute (and disgruntled citizen), copied more than seven thousand pages (or forty-seven volumes) of classified documents pertaining to the Vietnam War and demonstrating problematic messages sent to the American public by its leaders, including contradictory statements about the progress of the war directly from the president; these came to be known as the "Pentagon Papers." The documents illuminated a discord between the promises being made by politicians and the growing disenchantment of the American public growing weary of sending soldiers to fight a war that never seemed to end.

Some of the documents obtained by Ellsberg were secretly shared with and published, in part, by the *New York Times*. Publication of the documents ran the risk of violating the Espionage Act, which made it a crime for anyone to gain access to or use confidential U.S. defense information. After publishing portions of the papers within two editions of the daily paper, President Nixon requested the newspaper stop publishing the information, claiming it was causing "irreparable injury to the defense interests of the United States." An injunction was put in place that halted the *Times*' further publication of the paper, while simultaneously, the *Washington Post* had obtained and began publishing excerpts from the same documents. After facing hearings at both the trial and appeal levels seeking a determination of whether "freedom of the press" actually included publishing documents like these, the cases were combined and reached the steps of the U.S. Supreme Court in June 1971. The Court immediately heard oral arguments and issued a brief one-paragraph opinion within four days.

Consider the importance of a free press and the need for citizens of a country to receive accurate and timely information regarding national security and defense issues. Yet are there times when the government should have the ability to keep some information secret, particularly if the information protects the citizens?

Legal Issue

Does the First Amendment protect the press's ability to publish sensitive government documents?

Vocabulary

Injunction: a judicial order requiring an action to cease or stop
Judicial restraint: when a court (or judge) refrains from overreaching into areas of the law that may not be relevant to the case at hand
Equity jurisdiction: "Equitable jurisdiction is a system of justice designed to supplement the common law by taking action in a reasonable and fair manner which results in just outcome" (https://definitions.uslegal.com/e/equitable-jurisdiction/)
Per curiam: a unanimous decision by a court
Presumption: What is perceived to be true. In a court case, a presumption of innocence means the court will assume someone is innocent until otherwise proven to be guilty.

Parties in the Case

Petitioner: The *New York Times* newspaper
Respondent(s): The United States Government
    Edited version of case in the original language with distractors removed.

NEW YORK TIMES CO. V. UNITED STATES, 403 U.S. 713 (1971)

PER CURIAM

We granted certiorari in these cases in which the United States seeks to enjoin the *New York Times* and the *Washington Post* from publishing the contents of a classified study entitled "History of U.S. Decision-Making Process on Viet Nam Policy."

"Any system of prior restraints of expression comes to this Court bearing a heavy presumption against its constitutional validity." The government "thus carries a heavy burden of showing justification for the imposition of such a restraint." The District Court for the Southern District of New York, in the *New York Times* case, and the District Court for the District of Columbia and the Court of Appeals for the District of Columbia Circuit, in the *Washington Post* case, held that the Government had not met that burden. We agree.

The judgment of the Court of Appeals for the District of Columbia Circuit is therefore affirmed. The order of the Court of Appeals for the Second Circuit is reversed, and the case is remanded with directions to enter a judgment affirming the judgment of the District Court for the Southern District of New York. The stays entered June 25, 1971, by the Court are vacated. The judgments shall issue forthwith.

So ordered.

- *These few paragraphs were the entire opinion of the Court. That is, the government had not met its burden of justifying why suppression of the documents was necessary. What should be considered when weighing the burden of publication versus suppression of information to the American public?*

MR. JUSTICE BLACK, with whom MR. JUSTICE DOUGLAS joins, concurring.

I adhere to the view that the government's case against the *Washington Post* should have been dismissed, and that the injunction against the *New York Times* should have been vacated without oral argument when the cases were first presented to this Court. I believe that every moment's continuance of the injunctions against these newspapers amounts to a flagrant, indefensible, and continuing violation of the First Amendment. Furthermore, after oral argument, I agree completely that we must affirm the judgment of the Court of Appeals for the District of Columbia Circuit and reverse the judgment of the Court of Appeals for the Second Circuit for the reasons stated by my Brothers DOUGLAS and BRENNAN. In my view, it is unfortunate that some of my Brethren are apparently willing to hold that the publication of news may sometimes be enjoined. Such a holding would make a shambles of the First Amendment.

Our government was launched in 1789 with the adoption of the Constitution. The Bill of Rights, including the First Amendment, followed in 1791. Now, for the first time in the 182 years since the founding of the Republic, the federal courts are asked to hold that the First Amendment does not mean what it says, but rather means that the government can halt the publication of current news of vital importance to the people of this country.

In seeking injunctions against these newspapers, and in its presentation to the Court, the Executive Branch seems to have forgotten the essential purpose and history of the First Amendment. When the Constitution was adopted, many people strongly opposed it because the document contained no Bill of Rights to safeguard certain basic freedoms. They especially feared that the new powers granted to a central government might be interpreted to permit the government to curtail freedom of religion, press, assembly, and speech. In response to an overwhelming public clamor, James Madison offered a series of amendments to satisfy citizens that these great liberties would remain safe and beyond the power of government to abridge. Madison proposed what later became the First Amendment in three parts, two of which are set out below, and one of which proclaimed: "The people shall not be deprived or abridged of their right to speak, to write, or to publish their sentiments, *and the freedom of the press, as one of the great bulwarks of liberty, shall be inviolable.*"

The amendments were offered to curtail and restrict the general powers granted to the Executive, Legislative, and Judicial Branches two years before in the original Constitution. The Bill of Rights changed the original Constitution into a new charter under which no branch of government could abridge the people's freedoms of press, speech, religion, and assembly. Yet the Solicitor General argues and some members of the Court appear to agree that the general powers of the government adopted in the original Constitution should be interpreted to limit and restrict the specific and emphatic guarantees of the Bill of Rights adopted later. I can imagine no greater perversion of history. Madison and the other Framers of the First Amendment, able men that they were, wrote in language they earnestly believed could never be misunderstood: "Congress shall make no law . . . abridging the freedom . . . of the press. . . ." Both the history and language of the First Amendment support the view that the press must be left free to publish news, whatever the source, without censorship, injunctions, or prior restraints.

- *Should the Bill of Rights be interpreted or viewed as restricted by the government simply because the Amendments were adopted after the passage of the original Constitution?*

In the First Amendment, the founding fathers gave the free press the protection it must have to fulfill its essential role in our democracy. The press was to serve the governed, not the governors. The government's power to censor the press was abolished so that the press would remain forever free to censure the government. The press was protected so that it could bare the secrets of government and inform the people. Only a free and unrestrained press can effectively expose deception in government. And paramount among the responsibilities of a free press is the duty to prevent any part of the government from deceiving the people and sending them off to distant lands to die of foreign fevers and foreign shot and shell. In my view, far from deserving condemnation for their courageous reporting, the *New York Times*, the *Washington Post*, and other newspapers should be commended for serving the purpose that the Founding Fathers saw so clearly. In revealing the workings of government that led to the Vietnam war, the newspapers nobly did precisely that which the Founders hoped and trusted they would do.

In other words, we are asked to hold that, despite the First Amendment's emphatic command, the Executive Branch, the Congress, and the Judiciary can make laws enjoining publication of current news and abridging freedom of the press in the name of "national security." The government does not even attempt to rely on any act of Congress. Instead, it makes the bold and dangerously far-reaching contention that the courts should take it upon themselves to "make" a law abridging freedom of the press in the name of equity, presidential power and national security, even when the representatives of the people in Congress have adhered to the command of the First Amendment and refused to make such a law. To find that the president has "inherent power" to halt the publication of news by resort to the courts would wipe out the First Amendment and destroy the fundamental liberty and security of the very people the government hopes to make "secure." No one can read the history of the adoption of the First Amendment without being convinced beyond any doubt that it was injunctions like those sought here that Madison and his collaborators intended to outlaw in this Nation for all time.

- *Had Congress made a new law prohibiting the publication of these documents, would that have changed the outcome of this case?*

The word "security" is a broad, vague generality whose contours should not be invoked to abrogate the fundamental law embodied in the First Amendment. The guarding of military and diplomatic secrets at the expense of informed representative government provides no real security for our Republic. The framers of the First Amendment, fully aware of both the need to defend a new nation and the abuses of the English and Colonial governments, sought to give this new society strength and security by providing that freedom of speech, press, religion, and assembly should not be abridged. This thought was eloquently expressed in 1937 by Mr. Chief Justice Hughes—great man and great Chief Justice that he was—when the Court held a man could not be punished for attending a meeting run by Communists.

"The greater the importance of safeguarding the community from incitements to the overthrow of our institutions by force and violence, the more imperative is the need to preserve inviolate the constitutional rights of free speech, free press and free assembly in order to maintain the opportunity for free political discussion, to the end that government may be responsive to the will of the people and that changes, if desired, may be obtained by peaceful means. Therein lies the security of the Republic, the very foundation of constitutional government."

- *Why is security a national priority and how could publication of these documents interfere with the nation's security?*

MR. JUSTICE DOUGLAS, with whom MR. JUSTICE BLACK joins, concurring.

While I join the opinion of the Court, I believe it necessary to express my views more fully. It should be noted at the outset that the First Amendment provides that "Congress shall make no law . . . abridging the freedom of speech, or of the press." That leaves, in my view, no room for governmental restraint on the press. There is, moreover, no statute barring the publication by the press of the material which the *Times* and the *Post* seek to use. So any power that the government possesses must come from its "inherent power." These disclosures may have a serious impact. But that is no basis for sanctioning a previous restraint on the press. The government says that it has inherent powers to go into court and obtain an injunction to protect the national interest, which, in this case, is alleged to be national security.

The dominant purpose of the First Amendment was to prohibit the widespread practice of governmental suppression of embarrassing information. It is common knowledge that the First Amendment was adopted against the widespread use of the common law of seditious libel to punish the dissemination of material that is embarrassing to the powers-that-be. The present cases will, I think, go down in history as the most dramatic illustration of that principle. A debate of large proportions goes on in the Nation over our posture in Vietnam. That debate antedated the disclosure of the contents of the present documents. The latter are highly relevant to the debate in progress.

Secrecy in government is fundamentally anti-democratic, perpetuating bureaucratic errors. Open debate and discussion of public issues are vital to our national health. On public questions, there should be "uninhibited, robust, and wide-open" debate.

There are numerous sets of this material in existence, and they apparently are not under any controlled custody. Moreover, the president has sent a set to the Congress. We start, then, with a case where there already is rather wide distribution of the material that is destined for publicity, not secrecy. I have gone over the material listed in the *in camera* brief of the United States. It is all history, not future events. None of it is more recent than 1968.

- *Does the recent nature of the information within the documents, here described as being drafted several years before appearing before the Court, diminish the threat to national security? Why or why not?*

MR. JUSTICE STEWART, with whom MR. JUSTICE WHITE joins, concurring.

In the governmental structure created by our Constitution, the Executive is endowed with enormous power in the two related areas of national defense and international relations. This power, largely unchecked by the Legislative and Judicial branches, has been pressed to the very hilt since the advent of the nuclear missile age. For better or for worse, the simple fact is that a president of the United States possesses vastly greater constitutional independence in these two vital areas of power than does, say, a prime minister of a country with a parliamentary form of government.

In the absence of the governmental checks and balances present in other areas of our national life, the only effective restraint upon executive policy and power in the areas of national defense and international affairs may lie in an enlightened citizenry—in an informed and critical public opinion which alone can here protect the values of democratic government. For this reason, it is perhaps here that a press that is alert, aware, and free most vitally serves the basic purpose of the First Amendment. For, without an informed and free press, there cannot be an enlightened people.

- *What does it mean to have an "enlightened citizenry" and what conditions must be met to make that happen?*

Yet it is elementary that the successful conduct of international diplomacy and the maintenance of an effective national defense require both confidentiality and secrecy. Other nations can hardly deal with this Nation in an atmosphere of mutual trust unless they can be assured that their confidences will be kept. And, within our own executive departments, the development of considered and intelligent international policies would be impossible if those charged with their formulation could not communicate with each other freely, frankly, and in confidence. In the area of basic national defense, the frequent need for absolute secrecy is, of course, self-evident.

I think there can be but one answer to this dilemma, if dilemma it be. The responsibility must be where the power is. If the Constitution gives the Executive a large degree of unshared power in the conduct of foreign affairs and the maintenance of our national defense, then, under the Constitution, the Executive must have the largely unshared duty to determine and preserve the degree of internal security necessary to exercise that power successfully. It is an awesome responsibility, requiring judgment and wisdom of a high order. I should suppose that moral, political, and practical considerations would dictate that a very first principle of that wisdom would be an insistence upon avoiding secrecy for its own sake. For when everything is classified, then nothing is classified, and the system becomes one to be disregarded by the cynical or the careless, and to be manipulated by those intent on self-protection or self-promotion. I should suppose, in short, that the hallmark of a truly effective internal security system would be the maximum possible disclosure, recognizing that secrecy can best be preserved only when credibility is truly maintained. But, be that as it may, it is clear to me that it is the constitutional duty of the Executive—as a matter of sovereign prerogative, and not as a matter of law as the courts know law—through the promulgation and enforcement of executive regulations, to protect the confidentiality necessary to carry out its responsibilities in the fields of international relations and national defense.

But in the cases before us, we are asked neither to construe specific regulations nor to apply specific laws. We are asked, instead, to perform a function that the Constitution gave to the Executive, not the Judiciary. We are asked, quite simply, to prevent the publication by two newspapers of material that the Executive Branch insists should not, in the national interest, be published. I am convinced that the Executive is correct with respect to some of the documents involved. But I cannot say that disclosure of any of them will surely result in direct, immediate, and irreparable damage to our Nation or its people. That being so, there can under the First Amendment be but one judicial resolution of the issues before us. I join the judgments of the Court.

- *Justices Stewart and White seem to believe true power rests within the executive branch to determine what is truly damaging to the country and what is not. In light of this belief, what caused them to deny the government's request to stop publication?*

MR. JUSTICE WHITE, with whom MR. JUSTICE STEWART joins, concurring.

I concur in today's judgments, but only because of the concededly extraordinary protection against prior restraints enjoyed by the press under our constitutional system. I do not say that in no circumstances would the First Amendment permit an injunction against publishing information about government plans or operations. Nor, after examining the materials the government characterizes as the most sensitive and destructive, can I deny that revelation of these documents will do substantial damage to public interests. Indeed, I am confident that their disclosure will have that result. But I nevertheless agree that the United States has not satisfied the very heavy burden that it must meet to warrant an injunction against publication in these cases, at least in the absence of express and appropriately limited congressional authorization for prior restraints in circumstances such as these. . . . Moreover, because the material poses substantial dangers to national interests, and because of the hazards of criminal sanctions, a responsible press may choose never to publish the more sensitive materials. To sustain the government in these cases would start the courts down a long and hazardous road that I am not willing to travel, at least without congressional guidance and direction.

It is not easy to reject the proposition urged by the United States, and to deny relief on its good faith claims in these cases that publication will work serious damage to the country. But that discomfiture is considerably dispelled by the infrequency of prior-restraint cases. Normally, publication will occur and the damage be done before the government has either opportunity or grounds for suppression. So here, publication has already begun, and a substantial part of the threatened damage has already occurred. The fact of a massive breakdown in security is known, access to the documents by many unauthorized people is undeniable, and the efficacy of equitable relief against these or other newspapers to avert anticipated damage is doubtful, at best.

What is more, terminating the ban on publication of the relatively few sensitive documents the government now seeks to suppress does not mean that the law either requires or invites newspapers or others to publish them, or that they will be immune from criminal action if they do. Prior restraints require an unusually heavy justification under the First Amendment, but failure by the government to justify prior restraints does not measure its constitutional entitlement to a conviction for criminal publication. That the government mistakenly chose to proceed by injunction does not mean that it could not successfully proceed in another way.

Of course, in the cases before us, the unpublished documents have been demanded by the United States, and their import has been made known at least to counsel for the newspapers involved. It is thus clear that Congress has addressed itself to the problems of protecting the security of the country and the national defense from unauthorized disclosure of potentially damaging information. It has not, however, authorized the injunctive remedy against threatened publication. It has apparently been satisfied to rely on criminal sanctions and their deterrent effect on the responsible, as well as the irresponsible, press. I am not, of course, saying that either of these newspapers has yet committed a crime, or that either would commit a crime if it published all the material now in its possession. That matter must await resolution in the context of a criminal proceeding if one is instituted by the United States. In that event, the issue of guilt or innocence would be determined by procedures and standards quite different from those that have purported to govern these injunctive proceedings.

MR. JUSTICE MARSHALL, concurring.

The government contends that the only issue in these cases is whether, in a suit by the United States, "the First Amendment bars a court from prohibiting a newspaper from publishing material whose disclosure would pose a 'grave and immediate danger to the security of the United States.'" With all due respect, I believe the ultimate issue in these cases is even more basic than the one posed by the solicitor general. The issue is whether this Court or the Congress has the power to make law.

- *What is important about this question—whether the Court or the Congress has the power to make law? Why would this question arise in this case?*

In these cases, there is no problem concerning the president's power to classify information as "secret" or "top secret." Congress has specifically recognized presidential authority, which has been formally exercised in Executive Order 10501 (1953), to classify documents and information. Nor is there any issue here regarding the president's power as Chief Executive and Commander in Chief to protect national security by disciplining employees who disclose information and by taking precautions to prevent leaks.

The problem here is whether, in these particular cases, the Executive Branch has authority to invoke the equity jurisdiction of the courts to protect what it believes to be the national interest. The government argues that, in addition to the inherent power of any government to protect itself, the president's power to conduct foreign affairs and his position as commander in chief give him authority to impose censorship on the press to protect his ability to deal effectively with foreign nations and to conduct the military affairs of the country. Of course, it is beyond cavil that the president has broad powers by virtue of his primary responsibility for the conduct of our foreign affairs and his position as commander in chief.

On at least two occasions, Congress has refused to enact legislation that would have made the conduct engaged in here unlawful and given the president the power that he seeks in this case. In 1917, during the debate over the original Espionage Act, still the basic provisions of § 793, Congress rejected a proposal to give the president in time of war or threat of war authority to directly prohibit by proclamation the publication of information relating to national defense that might be useful to the enemy.

Congress rejected this proposal after war against Germany had been declared, even though many believed that there was a grave national emergency and that the threat of security leaks and espionage was serious. The Executive Branch has not gone to Congress and requested that the decision to provide such power be reconsidered. Instead, the Executive Branch comes to this Court and asks that it be granted the power Congress refused to give.

Either the government has the power under statutory grant to use traditional criminal law to protect the country or, if there is no basis for arguing that Congress has made the activity a crime, it is plain that Congress has specifically refused to grant the authority the government seeks from this Court. In either case, this Court does not have authority to grant the requested relief. It is not for this Court to fling itself into every breach perceived by some government official, nor is it for this Court to take on itself the burden of enacting law, especially a law that Congress has refused to pass.

MR. CHIEF JUSTICE BURGER, dissenting.

In these cases, the imperative of a free and unfettered press comes into collision with another imperative, the effective functioning of a complex modern government, and, specifically, the effective exercise of certain constitutional powers of the Executive. Only those who view the First Amendment as an absolute in all circumstances—a view I respect, but reject—can find such cases as these to be simple or easy.

These cases are not simple for another and more immediate reason. We do not know the facts of the cases. No District Judge knew all the facts. No Court of Appeals judge knew all the facts. No member of this Court knows all the facts.

Why are we in this posture, in which only those judges to whom the First Amendment is absolute and permits of no restraint in any circumstances or for any reason, are really in a position to act?

The newspapers make a derivative claim under the First Amendment; they denominate this right as the public "right to know"; by implication, the Times asserts a sole trusteeship of that right by virtue of its journalistic "scoop." The right is asserted as an absolute. Of course, the First Amendment right itself is not an absolute, as Justice Holmes so long ago pointed out in his aphorism concerning the right to shout "fire" in a crowded theater if there was no fire. Conceivably, such exceptions may be lurking in these cases and, would have been flushed had they been properly considered in the trial courts, free from unwarranted deadlines and frenetic pressures. An issue of this importance should be tried and heard in a judicial atmosphere conducive to thoughtful, reflective deliberation, especially when haste, in terms of hours, is unwarranted in light of the long period the *Times*, by its own choice, deferred publication.

- *Justice Burger is concerned about how quickly this case moved through the courts, including when it arrived at the Supreme Court. Why might this influence the outcome of the case?*

It is not disputed that the *Times* has had unauthorized possession of the documents for three to four months, during which it has had its expert analysts studying them, presumably digesting them and preparing the material for publication. During all of this time, the *Times*, presumably in its capacity as trustee of the public's "right to know," has held up publication for purposes it considered proper, and thus public knowledge was delayed. No doubt this was for a good reason; the analysis of 7,000 pages of complex material drawn from a vastly greater volume of material would inevitably take time, and the writing of good news stories takes time. But why should the United States Government, from whom this information was illegally acquired by someone, along with all the counsel, trial judges, and appellate judges be placed under needless pressure? After these months of deferral, the alleged "right to know" has somehow and suddenly become a right that must be vindicated instanter.

Would it have been unreasonable, since the newspaper could anticipate the government's objections to release of secret material, to give the government an opportunity to review the entire collection and determine whether agreement could be reached on publication? Stolen or not, if security was not, in fact, jeopardized, much of the material could no doubt have been declassified, since it spans a period ending in 1968. With such an approach— one that great newspapers have in the past practiced and stated editorially to be the duty of an honorable press—the newspapers and government might well have narrowed the area of disagreement as to what was and was not publishable, leaving the remainder to be resolved in orderly litigation, if necessary. To me, it is hardly believable that a newspaper long regarded as a great institution in American life would fail to perform one of the basic and simple duties of every citizen with respect to the discovery or possession of stolen property or secret government documents. That duty, I had thought— perhaps naively—was to report forthwith, to responsible public officers. This duty rests on taxi drivers, Justices, and the *New York Times*. The course followed by the *Times*, whether so calculated or not, removed any possibility of orderly litigation of the issue. If the action of the judges up to now has been correct, that result is sheer happenstance.

- *Did the* New York Times *have a duty to report its acquisition of stolen documents? Why or why not?*

The consequence of all this melancholy series of events is that we literally do not know what we are acting on. As I see it, we have been forced to deal with litigation concerning rights of great magnitude without an adequate record, and surely without time for adequate treatment either in the prior proceedings or in this Court. It is interesting to note that counsel on both sides, in oral argument before this Court, were frequently unable to respond to questions on factual points. Not surprisingly, they pointed out that they had been working literally "around the clock," and simply were unable to review the documents that give rise to these cases and were not familiar with them. This Court is in no better posture. I agree generally with MR. JUSTICE HARLAN and MR. JUSTICE BLACKMUN, but I am not prepared to reach the merits.

We all crave speedier judicial processes, but, when judges are pressured, as in these cases, the result is a parody of the judicial function. As noted elsewhere, the *Times* conducted its analysis of the 47 volumes of Government documents over a period of several months, and did so with a degree of security that a government might envy. Such security was essential, of course, to protect the enterprise from others. Meanwhile, the *Times* has copyrighted its material, and there were strong intimations in the oral argument that the *Times* contemplated enjoining its use by any other publisher in violation of its copyright. Paradoxically, this would afford it a protection, analogous to prior restraint, against all others—a protection the *Times* denies the government of the United States. Interestingly, the *Times* explained its refusal to allow the Government to examine its own purloined documents by saying in substance this might compromise *its* sources and informants! The Times thus asserts a right to guard the secrecy of its sources while denying that the government of the United States has that power.

With respect to the question of inherent power of the Executive to classify papers, records, and documents as secret, or otherwise unavailable for public exposure, and to secure aid of the courts for enforcement, there may be an analogy with respect to this Court. No statute gives this Court express power to establish and enforce the utmost security measures for the secrecy of our deliberations and records. Yet I have little doubt as to the inherent power of the Court to protect the confidentiality of its internal operations by whatever judicial measures may be required.

- *Consider this last paragraph of Justice Burger's dissent. How is the case at hand analogous to the internal workings of the Court? Should the executive branch be able to protect its internal workings with no interference from constitutional restraints?*

MR. JUSTICE HARLAN, with whom THE CHIEF JUSTICE and MR. JUSTICE BLACKMUN join, dissenting.

These cases forcefully call to mind the wise admonition of Mr. Justice Holmes, "Great cases, like hard cases, make bad law. For great cases are called great not by reason of their real importance in shaping the law of the future, but because of some accident of immediate overwhelming interest which appeals to the feelings and distorts the judgment. These immediate interests exercise a kind of hydraulic pressure which makes what previously was clear seem doubtful, and before which even well settled principles of law will bend." With all respect, I consider that the Court has been almost irresponsibly feverish in dealing with these cases.

Both the Court of Appeals for the Second Circuit and the Court of Appeals for the District of Columbia Circuit rendered judgment on June 23. The *New York Times'* petition for certiorari, its motion for accelerated consideration thereof, and its application for interim relief were filed in this Court on June 24 at about 11 a.m. The application of the United States for interim relief in the *Post* case was also filed here on June 24 at about 7:15 p.m. This Court's order setting a hearing before us on June 26 at 11 a.m., a course which I joined only to avoid the possibility of even more peremptory action by the Court, was issued less than 24 hours before. The record in the *Post* case was filed with the Clerk shortly before 1 p.m. on June 25; the record in the *Times* case did not arrive until 7 or 8 o'clock that same night. The briefs of the parties were received less than two hours before argument on June 26.

This frenzied train of events took place in the name of the presumption against prior restraints created by the First Amendment. Due regard for the extraordinarily important and difficult questions involved in these litigations should have led the Court to shun such a precipitate timetable.

The time which has been available to us, to the lower courts, and to the parties has been wholly inadequate for giving these cases the kind of consideration they deserve. It is a reflection on the stability of the judicial process that these great issues—as important as any that have arisen during my time on the Court—should have been decided under the pressures engendered by the torrent of publicity that has attended these litigations from their inception.

Forced as I am to reach the merits of these cases, I dissent from the opinion and judgments of the Court. Within the severe limitations imposed by the time constraints under which I have been required to operate, I can only state my reasons in telescoped form, even though, in different circumstances, I would have felt constrained to deal with the cases in the fuller sweep indicated above.

Even if there is some room for the judiciary to override the executive determination, it is plain that the scope of review must be exceedingly narrow. I can see no indication in the opinions of either the District Court or the Court of Appeals in the *Post* litigation that the conclusions of the Executive were given even the deference owing to an administrative agency, much less that owing to a co-equal branch of the Government operating within the field of its constitutional prerogative.

Accordingly, I would vacate the judgment of the Court of Appeals for the District of Columbia Circuit on this ground, and remand the case for further proceedings in the District Court. Before the commencement of such further proceedings, due opportunity should be afforded the Government for procuring from the Secretary of State or the Secretary of Defense or both an expression of their views on the issue of national security. The ensuing review by the District Court should be in accordance with the views expressed in this opinion. And, for the reasons stated above, I would affirm the judgment of the Court of Appeals for the Second Circuit.

Pending further hearings in each case conducted under the appropriate ground rules, I would continue the restraints on publication. I cannot believe that the doctrine prohibiting prior restraints reaches to the point of preventing courts from maintaining the *status quo* long enough to act responsibly in matters of such national importance as those involved here.

MR. JUSTICE BLACKMUN, dissenting.

I join MR. JUSTICE HARLAN in his dissent. I also am in substantial accord with much that MR. JUSTICE WHITE says, by way of admonition, in the latter part of his opinion.

At this point, the focus is on only the comparatively few documents specified by the Government as critical. So far as the other material—vast in amount—is concerned, let it be published and published forthwith if the newspapers, once the strain is gone and the sensationalism is eased, still feel the urge so to do.

But we are concerned here with the few documents specified from the 47 volumes. The *New York Times* clandestinely devoted a period of three months to examining the 47 volumes that came into its unauthorized possession. Once it had begun publication of material from those volumes, the *New York* case now before us emerged. It immediately assumed, and ever since has maintained, a frenetic pace and character. Seemingly, once publication started, the material could not be made public fast enough. Seemingly, from then on, every deferral or delay, by restraint or otherwise, was abhorrent, and was to be deemed violative of the First Amendment and of the public's "right immediately to know." Yet that newspaper stood before us at oral argument and professed criticism of the Government for not lodging its protest earlier than by a Monday telegram following the initial Sunday publication.

Two federal district courts, two United States courts of appeals, and this Court—within a period of less than three weeks from inception until today—have been pressed into hurried decision of profound constitutional issues on inadequately developed and largely assumed facts without the careful deliberation that, one would hope, should characterize the American judicial process. There has been much writing about the law and little knowledge and less digestion of the facts. In the *New York* case, the judges, both trial and appellate, had not yet examined the basic material when the case was brought here. In the District of Columbia case, little more was done, and what was accomplished in this respect was only on required remand, with the Washington Post, on the excuse that it was trying to protect its source of information, initially refusing to reveal what material it actually possessed, and with the District Court forced to make assumptions as to that possession.

With such respect as may be due to the contrary view, this, in my opinion, is not the way to try a lawsuit of this magnitude and asserted importance. It is not the way for federal courts to adjudicate, and to be required to adjudicate, issues that allegedly concern the Nation's vital welfare. The country would be none the worse off were the cases tried quickly, to be sure, but in the customary and properly deliberative manner. The most recent of the material, it is said, dates no later than 1968, already about three years ago, and the Times itself took three months to formulate its plan of procedure and, thus, deprived its public for that period.

I therefore would remand these cases to be developed expeditiously, of course, but on a schedule permitting the orderly presentation of evidence from both sides. I know from past personal experience the agony of time pressure in the preparation of litigation. But these cases and the issues involved and the courts, including this one, deserve better than has been produced thus far.

It may well be that, if these cases were allowed to develop as they should be developed, and to be tried as lawyers should try them and as courts should hear them, free of pressure and panic and sensationalism, other light would be shed on the situation, and contrary considerations, for me, might prevail. But that is not the present posture of the litigation.

The Court, however, decides the cases today the other way. I therefore add one final comment. I strongly urge, and sincerely hope, that these two newspapers will be fully aware of their ultimate responsibilities to the United States of America. Judge Wilkey, dissenting in the District of Columbia case, after a review of only the affidavits before his court (the basic papers had not then been made available by either party), concluded that there were a number of examples of documents that, if in the possession of the *Post* and if published, "could clearly result in great harm to the nation," and he defined "harm" to mean "the death of soldiers, the destruction of alliances, the greatly increased difficulty of negotiation with our enemies, the inability of our diplomats to negotiate."

I, for one, have now been able to give at least some cursory study not only to the affidavits, but to the material itself. I regret to say that, from this examination, I fear that Judge Wilkey's statements have possible foundation. I therefore share his concern. I hope that damage has not already been done. If, however, damage has been done, and if, with the Court's action today, these newspapers proceed to publish the critical documents and there results therefrom "the death of soldiers, the destruction of alliances, the greatly increased difficulty of negotiation with our enemies, the inability of our diplomats to negotiate," to which list I might add the factors of prolongation of the war and of further delay in the freeing of United States prisoners, then the Nation's people will know where the responsibility for these sad consequences rests.

Connecting, Arguing, and Analyzing the Case

1. Create a visual representation laying out the balance of power within this case. What reasons did the government have for halting publica-

tion? What rationale did the newspapers use to compel publication? How do we determine which "weighs" more?
2. In 1976, the U.S. Supreme Court heard the case *Nebraska Press Association v. Stuart* where the government sought to prevent the press from broadcasting confessions of an accused murderer. The Court there ruled that preventing the press from publication was a "prior restraint" and not permissible under the First Amendment. How were the facts of this case different than the ones in the *New York Times* case and what differentiates the two cases?
3. Compare the Court's ruling here to that in *Schenck* in chapter 3? Why are the outcomes different?
4. In 2018, President Donald Trump revoked the press pass of a CNN journalist, which barred him from entering White House press gatherings, because the president disagreed with his coverage of White House events. Does that action promote or discourage freedom of the press? Does the president hold the power to prevent access to certain news outlets or to support publication by only preferred news channels?

Chapter Ten

Wisconsin v. Yoder

The Free Exercise Clause found in the First Amendment of the U.S. Constitution states: "*Congress shall make no law respecting* an establishment of religion, *or prohibiting the free exercise* thereof; or abridging the freedom of speech, or of the press; or the right of the people peaceably to assemble, and to petition the government for a redress of grievances" (emphasis added).

Harkening back to Thomas Jefferson's idea that the Founders should build "a wall of separation between Church and State" (Jefferson's letter to the Danbury Baptists, 1802), the Constitution provides two different things in the free exercise clause. It protects the free expression of an individual's own religion *and* guarantees that the government will not prefer one religion over another religion or prefer religion over nonreligion.

Consideration of the free expression portion of the Free Exercise Clause did not come before the Supreme Court until the case *Reynolds v. United States*, decided in 1879, when the Court was asked to consider the constitutionality of the prosecution of polygamy in Utah under federal law. Since *Reynolds*, the Court has considered a variety of free expression cases coming from groups such as Jehovah's Witnesses, Seventh Day Adventists, and Native American religious expression. In 1963, the Supreme Court in *Sherbert v. Verner* held that a state must have a "compelling interest" to restrict religious-based activity. *Wisconsin v. Yoder*, decided in 1972, addressed whether a religiously neutral law is unconstitutional if it "unduly burdens the practice of religion."

Legal Issue

When can the government enforce or nullify a law that burdens an individual's ability to freely express his or her religious beliefs?

Vocabulary

Amish: "of or relating to a Christian religious group whose members settled in America chiefly in the 18th century and continue to live in a traditional way on farms" (Merriam-Webster)
Compulsory: mandatory
Secular: nonreligious; having no religious foundation
Assimilated: "to absorb into the cultural tradition of a population or group" (Merriam-Webster)
Idiosyncrasies: "an individualizing characteristic or quality" (Merriam-Webster)
Censure: "the act of blaming or condemning sternly" (Merriam-Webster)

Parties in the Case

Respondents: Jonas Yoder, Wallace Miller, and Aiden Yutzy (on behalf of their children)
Petitioner: The State of Wisconsin
Edited version of case in the original language with distractors removed.

WISCONSIN V. YODER, 406 U.S. 205 (1972)

MR. CHIEF JUSTICE BURGER delivered the opinion of the Court.

On petition of the State of Wisconsin, we granted the writ of certiorari in this case to review a decision of the Wisconsin Supreme Court holding that respondents' convictions of violating the state's compulsory school attendance law were invalid under the Free Exercise Clause of the First Amendment to the United States Constitution, made applicable to the states by the Fourteenth Amendment. For the reasons hereafter stated, we affirm the judgment of the Supreme Court of Wisconsin.

Respondents Jonas Yoder and Wallace Miller are members of the Old Order Amish religion, and respondent Adin Yutzy is a member of the Conservative Amish Mennonite Church. They and their families are residents of Green County, Wisconsin. Wisconsin's compulsory school attendance law required them to cause their children to attend public or private school until reaching age 16, but the respondents declined to send their children, ages 14 and 15, to public school after they completed the eighth grade. The children were not enrolled in any private school, or within any recognized exception to the compulsory attendance law, and they are conceded to be subject to the Wisconsin statute.

- *What is the state's interest in requiring children to go to school? What are the parents' interests in not sending them to school?*

- *In this case, the parents are exerting their constitutional rights over their children. Should the desires of the children play a part in the Court's decision?*

On complaint of the school district administrator for the public schools, respondents were charged, tried, and convicted of violating the compulsory attendance law in Green County Court, and were fined the sum of $5 each. Respondents defended on the ground that the application of the compulsory attendance law violated their rights under the First and Fourteenth Amendments. The trial testimony showed that respondents believed, in accordance with the tenets of Old Order Amish communities generally, that their children's attendance at high school, public or private, was contrary to the Amish religion and way of life. They believed that, by sending their children to high school, they would not only expose themselves to the danger of the censure of the church community, but, as found by the county court, also endanger their own salvation and that of their children. The state stipulated that respondents' religious beliefs were sincere.

- *Make a list of the state's reasons for requiring education. Make a list of the individuals'—the Amish—reasons for not wanting to educate their children past the eighth grade?*
- *How does the Court judge the sincerity of one's beliefs?*

In support of their position, respondents presented as expert witnesses scholars on religion and education whose testimony is uncontradicted. They expressed their opinions on the relationship of the Amish belief concerning school attendance to the more general tenets of their religion, and described the impact that compulsory high school attendance could have on the continued survival of Amish communities as they exist in the United States today.

A related feature of Old Order Amish communities is their devotion to a life in harmony with nature and the soil, as exemplified by the simple life of the early Christian era that continued in America during much of our early national life.

Once a child has learned basic reading, writing, and elementary mathematics, these traits, skills, and attitudes admittedly fall within the category of those best learned through example and "doing," rather than in a classroom. And, at this time in life, the Amish child must also grow in his faith and his relationship to the Amish community if he is to be prepared to accept the heavy obligations imposed by adult baptism. In short, high school attendance with teachers who are not of the Amish faith—and may even be hostile to it—interposes a serious barrier to the integration of the Amish child into the Amish religious community.

The Amish do not object to elementary education through the first eight grades as a general proposition, because they agree that their children must have basic skills in the "three R's" in order to read the Bible, to be good farmers and citizens, and to be able to deal with non-Amish people when necessary in the course of daily affairs. They view such a basic education as acceptable because it does not significantly expose their children to worldly values or interfere with their development in the Amish community during the crucial adolescent period.

- *How much should the fact that the Court views the Amish people as "good" play a part in its decision?*

I

There is no doubt as to the power of a state, having a high responsibility for education of its citizens, to impose reasonable regulations for the control and duration of basic education. Thus, a state's interest in universal education, however highly we rank it, is not totally free from a balancing process when it impinges on fundamental rights and interests, such as those specifically protected by the Free Exercise Clause of the First Amendment, and the traditional interest of parents with respect to the religious upbringing of their children so long as they, in the words of *Pierce v. Society of Sisters*, "prepare [them] for additional obligations."

It follows that, in order for Wisconsin to compel school attendance beyond the eighth grade against a claim that such attendance interferes with the practice of a legitimate religious belief, it must appear either that the state does not deny the free exercise of religious belief by its requirement or that there is a state interest of sufficient magnitude to override the interest claiming protection under the Free Exercise Clause. Long before there was general acknowledgment of the need for universal formal education, the Religion Clauses had specifically and firmly fixed the right to free exercise of religious beliefs, and buttressing this fundamental right was an equally firm, even if less explicit, prohibition against the establishment of any religion by government. The values underlying these two provisions relating to religion have been zealously protected, sometimes even at the expense of other interests of admittedly high social importance.

- *What is the standard the Court imposes on the state to deny the free exercise of a legitimate religious belief? Do you agree with the rationale for the preference to free exercise the Court is giving in this section?*

II

We come then to the quality of the claims of the respondents concerning the alleged encroachment of Wisconsin's compulsory school attendance statute on their rights and the rights of their children to the free exercise of the religious beliefs they and their forebears have adhered to for almost three centuries. In evaluating those claims, we must be careful to determine whether the Amish religious faith and their mode of life are, as they claim, inseparable and interdependent. A way of life, however virtuous and admirable, may not be interposed as a barrier to reasonable state regulation of education if it is based on purely secular considerations; to have the protection of the Religion Clauses, the claims must be rooted in religious belief.

The conclusion is inescapable that secondary schooling, by exposing Amish children to worldly influences in terms of attitudes, goals, and values contrary to beliefs, and by substantially interfering with the religious development of the Amish child and his integration into the way of life of the Amish faith community at the crucial adolescent stage of development, contravenes the basic religious tenets and practice of the Amish faith, both as to the parent and the child.

The impact of the compulsory attendance law on respondents' practice of the Amish religion is not only severe, but inescapable, for the Wisconsin law affirmatively compels them, under threat of criminal sanction, to perform acts undeniably at odds with fundamental tenets of their religious beliefs.

In sum, the unchallenged testimony of acknowledged experts in education and religious history, almost 300 years of consistent practice, and strong evidence of a sustained faith pervading and regulating respondents' entire mode of life support the claim that enforcement of the state's requirement of compulsory formal education after the eighth grade would gravely endanger, if not destroy, the free exercise of respondents' religious beliefs.

- *Why does it matter that this religious sect is more than three hundred years old? The Supreme Court refers to this time and again in its decision. What if the Amish religion had only been fifteen years old? Should the age of a person's belief system make a difference?*

III

Wisconsin concedes that, under the Religion Clauses, religious beliefs are absolutely free from the state's control, but it argues that "actions," even though religiously grounded, are outside the protection of the First Amendment. But our decisions have rejected the idea that religiously grounded conduct is always outside the protection of the Free Exercise Clause. It is true that activities of individuals, even when religiously based, are often subject to regulation by the states in the exercise of their undoubted power to promote the health, safety, and general welfare, or the Federal Government in the exercise of its delegated powers. This case, therefore, does not become easier because respondents were convicted for their "actions" in refusing to send their children to the public high school; in this context, belief and action cannot be neatly confined in logic-tight compartments.

Nor can this case be disposed of on the grounds that Wisconsin's requirement for school attendance to age 16 applies uniformly to all citizens of the state and does not, on its face, discriminate against religions or a particular religion, or that it is motivated by legitimate secular concerns. A regulation neutral on its face may, in its application, nonetheless offend the constitutional requirement for governmental neutrality if it unduly burdens the free exercise of religion.

We turn, then, to the state's broader contention that its interest in its system of compulsory education is so compelling that even the established religious practices of the Amish must give way. Where fundamental claims of religious freedom are at stake, however, we cannot accept such a sweeping claim; despite its admitted validity in the generality of cases, we must searchingly examine the interests that the state seeks to promote by its requirement for compulsory education to age 16, and the impediment to those objectives that would flow from recognizing the claimed Amish exemption.

The state advances two primary arguments in support of its system of compulsory education. It notes, as Thomas Jefferson pointed out early in our history, that some degree of education is necessary to prepare citizens to participate effectively and intelligently in our open political system if we are to preserve freedom and independence. Further, education prepares individuals to be self-reliant and self-sufficient participants in society. We accept these propositions.

- *States are allowed to determine their own ages for compulsory education. Should every state be required to have the same requirements for compulsory education?*

However, the evidence adduced by the Amish in this case is persuasively to the effect that an additional one or two years of formal high school for Amish children in place of their long-established program of informal vocational education would do little to serve those interests. Respondents' experts testified at trial, without challenge, that the value of all education must be assessed in terms of its capacity to prepare the child for life. It is one thing to say that compulsory education for a year or two beyond the eighth grade may be necessary when its goal is the preparation of the child for life in modern society as the majority live, but it is quite another if the goal of education be viewed as the preparation of the child for life in the separated agrarian community that is the keystone of the Amish faith.

IV

Finally, the state, on authority of *Prince v. Massachusetts*, argues that a decision exempting Amish children from the state's requirement fails to recognize the substantive right of the Amish child to a secondary education, and fails to give due regard to the power of the state as *parens patriae* to extend the benefit of secondary education to children regardless of the wishes of their parents.

This case, of course, is not one in which any harm to the physical or mental health of the child or to the public safety, peace, order, or welfare has been demonstrated or may be properly inferred. The record is to the contrary, and any reliance on that theory would find no support in the evidence.

- *The Court refers to the state of Wisconsin acting as parens patriae. What does that mean? How much right should a state have to interfere with decisions of parents in raising their children? Should a state be allowed to step in for issues such as what chores a young person must do at home? Caring for younger siblings? Whether a young person receives vaccines and medical care? What do you think the line is for involvement from the state?*

V

For the reasons stated we hold, with the Supreme Court of Wisconsin, that the First and Fourteenth Amendments prevent the state from compelling respondents to cause their children to attend formal high school to age 16.

Affirmed.

MR. JUSTICE POWELL and MR. JUSTICE REHNQUIST took no part in the consideration or decision of this case.

Connecting, Arguing, and Analyzing the Case

1. Discuss how citizens should balance laws of the state against the personal rights and freedoms of the individual. For example, our society places a high priority on the right to have your body free from the invasive touch of other people, yet since 9/11, all people who fly on commercial airlines are subject to screenings where items of clothing may have to be removed and your body may be patted down. Why is this okay? Are there any people who should be allowed to have an exemption from this type of screening?

2. Five different organizations filed amicus curiae briefs to the Supreme Court about this case. An amicus curiae brief is a written submission to the Court by a party not directly involved in the case but who believes there is important information that the Court should hear from them about the case to help the Court make its decision. Write your own amicus brief where you give your reasoning to support either the petitioner's or respondent's point of view from your own experience.
3. Consider the case of a government employee responsible for issuing marriage licenses to couples seeking to wed within the county where she works. One particular employee, Jan, practices a religion that does not endorse marriage between two same-sex individuals. A same-sex couple show up at her office and ask to apply for a marriage license. Jan refuses to issue the license and claims it violates her "free exercise of religion" under the Establishment Clause because her signature would appear on the license permitting the marriage to be official. Does requiring Jan to issue the license unduly burden the practice of her religion?
4. Air Force Officer Goldman, an Orthodox Jew and ordained rabbi, was not allowed to wear his yarmulke while on duty or in his uniform. The Air Force regulation stated that headgear could not be worn "except by security police in the performance of their duties." A lawsuit was filed by Goldman alleging that the Air Force regulation violated the Constitution by preventing him from practicing his religion. The petitioner argued that the regulation, as applied to him, prohibited religiously motivated conduct. In the ensuing case, *Goldman v. Weinberger* (1986), the Supreme Court held in a 5-4 decision that no constitutional violation existed. The majority opinion stated that in this situation such practices as wearing a yarmulke would detract from uniformity desired in dress regulations, which was in the interest of the military.

   a. Identify the constitutional clause that is common to both *Goldman v. Weinberger* (1986) and *Wisconsin v. Yoder* (1972).
   b. Based on the constitutional clause identified in part a, explain why the facts of *Wisconsin v. Yoder* (1972) led to a similar holding in *Goldman v. Weinberger* (1986).
   c. Describe an action that members of the military who disagree with the holding in *Goldman v. Weinberger* (1986) could take to limit its impact.

Chapter Eleven

Roe v. Wade

The right to privacy is:

1) The right not to have one's personal matters disclosed or publicized; the right to be left alone. 2) The right against undue government intrusion into fundamental personal issues and decisions. Although the U.S. Constitution does not explicitly state that there is a right to privacy, Supreme Court decisions have found an implicit constitutional right to privacy in striking down laws that criminalize sodomy, the use of contraceptives, and abortion. (NOLO Dictionary, https://www.nolo.com/dictionary/right-to-privacy-term.html)

The First, Third, Fourth, Fifth, Ninth, and Fourteenth Amendments provide some protections for the right to privacy. The U.S. Supreme Court recognized an explicit right to privacy in the 1965 case *Griswold v. Connecticut*. The Court held that a law preventing access to contraceptives was unconstitutional because it violated a married couple's right to privacy because by interfering with their family decision making. "To hold that a right so basic and fundamental and so deep-rooted in our society as the right of privacy in marriage may be infringed because that right is not guaranteed in so many words by the first eight amendments to the Constitution is to ignore the Ninth Amendment, and to give it no effect whatsoever" (*Griswold v. Connecticut*). The recognition of this right set a lead for *Roe v. Wade*.

Legal Issue

Does a woman have a constitutional right to an abortion?

Vocabulary from the Case

Predilection: bias or preference

Admonition: warning with authority
Procure: to obtain
Vintage: time/age something happened
Proscribing: forbidding
Pseudonym: false name
Penumbras: rights that are implied from the rights explicitly protected in the Bill of Rights

Parties in the Case

Petitioner: Jane Roe, a Texas resident
Respondent: Henry Wade, the district attorney of Dallas County
Edited version of case in the original language with distractors removed.

ROE V. WADE, 410 U.S. 113 (1973)

MR. JUSTICE BLACKMUN delivered the opinion of the Court.
 This Texas federal appeal present[s] constitutional challenges to state criminal abortion legislation. The Texas statutes under attack here are typical of those that have been in effect in many States for approximately a century.
 [The Court mentions the case *Doe v. Bolton*, which was released the same day and overturned a Georgia abortion law.]
 We forthwith acknowledge our awareness of the sensitive and emotional nature of the abortion controversy, of the vigorous opposing views, even among physicians, and of the deep and seemingly absolute convictions that the subject inspires. One's philosophy, one's experiences, one's exposure to the raw edges of human existence, one's religious training, one's attitudes toward life and family and their values, and the moral standards one establishes and seeks to observe, are all likely to influence and to color one's thinking and conclusions about abortion. In addition, population growth, pollution, poverty, and racial overtones tend to complicate and not to simplify the problem.

- *The Court recognizes the humanity and complexity of the issue immediately. Why does the Court feel this is important?*

Our task, of course, is to resolve the issue by constitutional measurement, free of emotion and of predilection. We seek earnestly to do this, and, because we do, we have inquired into, and in this opinion place some emphasis upon, medical and medical-legal history and what that history reveals about man's attitudes toward the abortion procedure over the centuries. We bear in mind, too, Mr. Justice Holmes' admonition in his now-vindicated dissent in *Lochner v. New York*:

"[The Constitution] is made for people of fundamentally differing views, and the accident of our finding certain opinions natural and familiar or novel and even shocking ought not to conclude our judgment upon the question whether statutes embodying them conflict with the Constitution of the United States."

- *How does this contradict what the Court just said in the preceding paragraph?*

I

The Texas statutes that concern us here make it a crime to "procure an abortion," or to attempt one, except with respect to "an abortion procured or attempted by medical advice for the purpose of saving the life of the mother" [statute enacted in 1854]. Similar statutes are in existence in a majority of the States.

- *What is the law that is in question?*

II

Jane Roe, a single woman who was residing in Dallas County, Texas, instituted this federal action in March 1970, against the District Attorney of the county. She sought a declaratory judgment that the Texas criminal abortion statutes were unconstitutional on their face, and an injunction restraining the defendant from enforcing the statutes.

- *What does Jane Roe want?*

Roe alleged that she was unmarried and pregnant; that she wished to terminate her pregnancy by an abortion "performed by a competent, licensed physician, under safe, clinical conditions"; that she was unable to get a "legal" abortion in Texas because her life did not appear to be threatened by the continuation of her pregnancy; and that she could not afford to travel to another jurisdiction in order to secure a legal abortion under safe conditions. She claimed that the Texas statutes abridged her right of personal privacy, protected by the First, Fourth, Fifth, Ninth, and Fourteenth Amendments. By an amendment to her complaint, Roe purported to sue "on behalf of herself and all other women" similarly situated. [She also claimed the statues were unconstitutionally vague, but the Court does not need to go on to decide that issue.]

- *What constitutional right is Roe claiming?*

[T]he District Court held that the "fundamental right of single women and married persons to choose whether to have children is protected by the Ninth Amendment, through the Fourteenth Amendment," and that the Texas criminal abortion statutes were void on their face because they were both unconstitutionally vague and constituted an overbroad infringement of the plaintiffs' Ninth Amendment rights. The court then held that abstention was warranted with respect to the requests for an injunction.

- *Where did the district court find this constitutional right?*

[James Hubert Hallford, a licensed physician, who had previously been arrested for violations of the Texas abortion statues, and John and Mary Doe, a childless married couple, had joined the action, but the U.S. Supreme Court determined that neither of these parties had standing.]

IV

We are next confronted with issues of justiciability, standing, and abstention.

A. *Jane Roe.* Despite the use of the pseudonym, no suggestion is made that Roe is a fictitious person. For purposes of her case, we accept as true, and as established, her existence; her pregnant state, as of the inception of her suit in March 1970 and as late as May 21 of that year when she filed an alias affidavit with the District Court; and her inability to obtain a legal abortion in Texas.

Viewing Roe's case as of the time of its filing and thereafter until as late as May, there can be little dispute that it then presented a case or controversy and that, wholly apart from the class aspects, she, as a pregnant single woman thwarted by the Texas criminal abortion laws, had standing to challenge those statutes. Indeed, we do not read the appellee's brief as really asserting anything to the contrary. The "logical nexus between the status asserted and the claim sought to be adjudicated" and the necessary degree of contentiousness are both present.

The appellee notes, however, that the record does not disclose that Roe was pregnant at the time of the District Court hearing on May 22, 1970, or on the following June 17 when the court's opinion and judgment were filed. And he suggests that Roe's case must now be moot because she and all other members of her class are no longer subject to any 1970 pregnancy. The usual rule in federal cases is that an actual controversy must exist at stages of appellate or certiorari review, and not simply at the date the action is initiated.

But when, as here, pregnancy is a significant fact in the litigation, the normal 266-day human gestation period is so short that the pregnancy will come to term before the usual appellate process is complete. If that termination makes a case moot, pregnancy litigation seldom will survive much beyond the trial stage, and appellate review will be effectively denied. Our law should not be that rigid. Pregnancy often comes more than once to the same woman, and in the general population, if man is to survive, it will always be with us. Pregnancy provides a classic justification for a conclusion of nonmootness. It truly could be "capable of repetition, yet evading review."

We, therefore, agree with the District Court that Jane Roe had standing to undertake this litigation, that she presented a justiciable controversy, and that the termination of her 1970 pregnancy has not rendered her case moot.

- *Standing is the right for a party to bring a lawsuit. Why does the appellee challenge Roe's standing? What is the Court's justification of its decision that Roe does have standing?*

V

The principal thrust of appellant's attack on the Texas statutes is that they improperly invade a right, said to be possessed by the pregnant woman, to choose to terminate her pregnancy. Appellant would discover this right in the concept of personal "liberty" embodied in the Fourteenth Amendment's Due Process Clause; or in personal, marital, familial, and sexual privacy said to be protected by the Bill of Rights or its penumbras. Before addressing this claim, we feel it desirable briefly to survey, in several aspects, the history of abortion, for such insight as that history may afford us, and then to examine the state purposes and interests behind the criminal abortion laws.

VI

It perhaps is not generally appreciated that the restrictive criminal abortion laws in effect in a majority of states today are of relatively recent vintage. Those laws, generally proscribing abortion or its attempt at any time during pregnancy except when necessary to preserve the pregnant woman's life, are not of ancient or even of common law origin. Instead, they derive from statutory changes effected, for the most part, in the latter half of the nineteenth century.

Opinion of the Court Conference has appended an enlightening Prefatory Note.

- *In VI of the opinion, the Court discusses the following: ancient attitudes, the Hippocratic Oath, the common law, English statutory law, the American law, the position of the American Medical Association, the position of the American Public Health Association, and the position of the*

American Bar Association. Why would the Court discuss the history and various organizations' positions?

VII

Three reasons have been advanced to explain historically the enactment of criminal abortion laws in the nineteenth century and to justify their continued existence. It has been argued occasionally that these laws were the product of a Victorian social concern to discourage illicit sexual conduct. Texas, however, does not advance this justification in the present case, and it appears that no court or commentator has taken the argument seriously. The appellants contend, moreover, that this is not a proper state purpose, at all and suggest that, if it were, the Texas statutes are overbroad in protecting it, since the law fails to distinguish between married and unwed mothers.

A second reason is concerned with abortion as a medical procedure. When most criminal abortion laws were first enacted, the procedure was a hazardous one for the woman. This was particularly true prior to the development of antisepsis. Antiseptic techniques, of course, were based on discoveries by Lister, Pasteur, and others first announced in 1867, but were not generally accepted and employed until about the turn of the century. Abortion mortality was high. Even after 1900, and perhaps until as late as the development of antibiotics in the 1940s, standard modern techniques such as dilation and curettage were not nearly so safe as they are today. Thus, it has been argued that a state's real concern in enacting a criminal abortion law was to protect the pregnant woman, that is, to restrain her from submitting to a procedure that placed her life in serious jeopardy.

Modern medical techniques have altered this situation. Appellants and various *amici* refer to medical data indicating that abortion in early pregnancy, that is, prior to the end of the first trimester, although not without its risk, is now relatively safe. Mortality rates for women undergoing early abortions, where the procedure is legal, appear to be as low as or lower than the rates for normal childbirth. Consequently, any interest of the state in protecting the woman from an inherently hazardous procedure, except when it would be equally dangerous for her to forgo it, has largely disappeared. Of course, important state interests in the areas of health and medical standards do remain.

The state has a legitimate interest in seeing to it that abortion, like any other medical procedure, is performed under circumstances that insure maximum safety for the patient. This interest obviously extends at least to the performing physician and his staff, to the facilities involved, to the availability of after-care, and to adequate provision for any complication or emergency that might arise. The prevalence of high mortality rates at illegal "abortion mills" strengthens, rather than weakens, the state's interest in regulating the conditions under which abortions are performed. Moreover, the risk to the woman increases as her pregnancy continues. Thus, the state retains a definite interest in protecting the woman's own health and safety when an abortion is proposed at a late stage of pregnancy.

The third reason is the state's interest—some phrase it in terms of duty—in protecting prenatal life. Some of the argument for this justification rests on the theory that a new human life is present from the moment of conception. The state's interest and general obligation to protect life then extends, it is argued, to prenatal life. Only when the life of the pregnant mother herself is at stake, balanced against the life she carries within her, should the interest of the embryo or fetus not prevail. Logically, of course, a legitimate state interest in this area need not stand or fall on acceptance of the belief that life begins at conception or at some other point prior to live birth. In assessing the state's interest, recognition may be given to the less rigid claim that as long as at least potential life is involved, the state may assert interests beyond the protection of the pregnant woman alone.

Parties challenging state abortion laws have sharply disputed in some courts the contention that a purpose of these laws, when enacted, was to protect prenatal life. Pointing to the absence of legislative history to support the contention, they claim that most state laws were designed solely to protect the woman. Because medical advances have lessened this concern, at least with respect to abortion in early pregnancy, they argue that with respect to such abortions the laws can no longer be justified by any state interest. There is some scholarly support for this view of original purpose. The few state courts called upon to interpret their laws in the late nineteenth and early twentieth centuries did focus on the state's interest in protecting the woman's health, rather than in preserving the embryo and fetus. Proponents of this view point out that in many states, including Texas, by statute or judicial interpretation, the pregnant woman herself could not be prosecuted for self-abortion or for cooperating in an abortion performed upon her by another. They claim that adoption of the "quickening" distinction through received common law and state statutes tacitly recognizes the greater health hazards inherent in late abortion and impliedly repudiates the theory that life begins at conception.

It is with these interests that this case is concerned.

- *What are the three reasons for criminal abortion laws according to the Court? What are the interests with which the Court is concerned?*

VIII

The Constitution does not explicitly mention any right of privacy. In a line of decisions, however, going back perhaps as far as *Union Pacific R. Co. v.*

Botsford, the Court has recognized that a right of personal privacy, or a guarantee of certain areas or zones of privacy, does exist under the Constitution. In varying contexts, the Court or individual Justices have, indeed, found at least the roots of that right in the First Amendment.

This right of privacy, whether it be founded in the Fourteenth Amendment's concept of personal liberty and restrictions upon state action, as we feel it is, or, as the District Court determined, in the Ninth Amendment's reservation of rights to the people, is broad enough to encompass a woman's decision whether or not to terminate her pregnancy. The detriment that the state would impose upon the pregnant woman by denying this choice altogether is apparent. Specific and direct harm medically diagnosable even in early pregnancy may be involved. Maternity, or additional offspring, may force upon the woman a distressful life and future. Psychological harm may be imminent. Mental and physical health may be taxed by child care. There is also the distress, for all concerned, associated with the unwanted child, and there is the problem of bringing a child into a family already unable, psychologically and otherwise, to care for it. In other cases, as in this one, the additional difficulties and continuing stigma of unwed motherhood may be involved. All these are factors the woman and her responsible physician necessarily will consider in consultation.

- *What factors does the Court consider in identifying this "right to privacy"?*

On the basis of elements such as these, appellant and some *amici* argue that the woman's right is absolute and that she is entitled to terminate her pregnancy at whatever time, in whatever way, and for whatever reason she alone chooses. With this we do not agree. Appellant's arguments that Texas either has no valid interest at all in regulating the abortion decision, or no interest strong enough to support any limitation upon the woman's sole determination, are unpersuasive. The Court's decisions recognizing a right of privacy also acknowledge that some state regulation in areas protected by that right is appropriate. As noted above, a state may properly assert important interests in safeguarding health, in maintaining medical standards, and in protecting potential life. At some point in pregnancy, these respective interests become sufficiently compelling to sustain regulation of the factors that govern the abortion decision. The privacy right involved, therefore, cannot be said to be absolute. In fact, it is not clear to us that the claim asserted by some *amici* that one has an unlimited right to do with one's body as one pleases bears a close relationship to the right of privacy previously articulated in the Court's decisions.

- *What are the interests of the state?*

We, therefore, conclude that the right of personal privacy includes the abortion decision, but that this right is not unqualified, and must be considered against important state interests in regulation.

- *Make a chart comparing the interests of the woman and the interests of the state.*

Where certain "fundamental rights" are involved, the Court has held that regulation limiting these rights may be justified only by a "compelling state interest," *Kramer v. Union Free School District.*

- *Brainstorm what "compelling state interests" might be in preventing a woman from getting an abortion.*

IX

The District Court held that the appellee failed to meet his burden of demonstrating that the Texas statute's infringement upon Roe's rights was necessary to support a compelling state interest, and that, although the appellee presented "several compelling justifications for state presence in the area of abortions," the statutes outstripped these justifications and swept "far beyond any areas of compelling state interest." Appellant and appellee both contest that holding. Appellant, as has been indicated, claims an absolute right that bars any state imposition of criminal penalties in the area. Appellee argues that the state's determination to recognize and protect prenatal life from and after conception constitutes a compelling state interest. As noted above, we do not agree fully with either formulation.

- *Both the appellee and the appellant are contesting the district court rulings. How do they disagree?*

A. The appellee and certain *amici* argue that the fetus is a "person" within the language and meaning of the Fourteenth Amendment. In support of this, they outline at length and in detail the well known facts of fetal development. If this suggestion of personhood is established, the appellant's case, of course, collapses, for the fetus' right to life would then be guaranteed specifically by the Amendment. The appellant conceded as much on reargument. On the other hand, the appellee conceded on reargument that no case could be cited that holds that a fetus is a person within the meaning of the Fourteenth Amendment.

The Constitution does not define "person" in so many words. Section 1 of the Fourteenth Amendment contains three references to "person." The first, in defining "citizens," speaks of "persons born or naturalized in the United

States." The word also appears both in the Due Process Clause and in the Equal Protection Clause.

All this, together with our observation, that, throughout the major portion of the nineteenth century, prevailing legal abortion practices were far freer than they are today, persuades us that the word "person," as used in the Fourteenth Amendment, does not include the unborn.

This conclusion, however, does not of itself fully answer the contentions raised by Texas, and we pass on to other considerations.

- *Is an unborn included in the Fourteenth Amendment's protections? What is the Court's justification for this?*

B. The pregnant woman cannot be isolated in her privacy. She carries an embryo and, later, a fetus, if one accepts the medical definitions of the developing young in the human uterus. The situation therefore is inherently different from marital intimacy. As we have intimated above, it is reasonable and appropriate for a state to decide that, at some point in time another interest, that of health of the mother or that of potential human life, becomes significantly involved. The woman's privacy is no longer sole and any right of privacy she possesses must be measured accordingly.

Texas urges that, apart from the Fourteenth Amendment, life begins at conception and is present throughout pregnancy, and that, therefore, the state has a compelling interest in protecting that life from and after conception. We need not resolve the difficult question of when life begins. When those trained in the respective disciplines of medicine, philosophy, and theology are unable to arrive at any consensus, the judiciary, at this point in the development of man's knowledge, is not in a position to speculate as to the answer.

It should be sufficient to note briefly the wide divergence of thinking on this most sensitive and difficult question. There has always been strong support for the view that life does not begin until live birth. This was the belief of the Stoics. It appears to be the predominant, though not the unanimous, attitude of the Jewish faith. It may be taken to represent also the position of a large segment of the Protestant community, insofar as that can be ascertained; organized groups that have taken a formal position on the abortion issue have generally regarded abortion as a matter for the conscience of the individual and her family. As we have noted, the common law found greater significance in quickening. Physicians and their scientific colleagues have regarded that event with less interest and have tended to focus either upon conception, upon live birth, or upon the interim point at which the fetus becomes "viable," that is, potentially able to live outside the mother's womb, albeit with artificial aid. Viability is usually placed at about seven months (28 weeks) but may occur earlier, even at 24 weeks.

In areas other than criminal abortion, the law has been reluctant to endorse any theory that life, as we recognize it, begins before live birth, or to accord legal rights to the unborn except in narrowly defined situations and except when the rights are contingent upon live birth. For example, the traditional rule of tort law denied recovery for prenatal injuries even though the child was born alive. That rule has been changed in almost every jurisdiction. In most states, recovery is said to be permitted only if the fetus was viable, or at least quick, when the injuries were sustained, though few courts have squarely so held. In a recent development, generally opposed by the commentators, some states permit the parents of a stillborn child to maintain an action for wrongful death because of prenatal injuries. Such an action, however, would appear to be one to vindicate the parents' interest and is thus consistent with the view that the fetus, at most, represents only the potentiality of life. Similarly, unborn children have been recognized as acquiring rights or interests by way of inheritance or other devolution of property, and have been represented by guardians *ad litem*. Perfection of the interests involved, again, has generally been contingent upon live birth. In short, the unborn have never been recognized in the law as persons in the whole sense.

- *Why is the woman's right not absolute in her pregnancy?*

X

In view of all this, we do not agree that, by adopting one theory of life, Texas may override the rights of the pregnant woman that are at stake. We repeat, however, that the State does have an important and legitimate interest in preserving and protecting the health of the pregnant woman, whether she be a resident of the State or a nonresident who seeks medical consultation and treatment there, and that it has still *another* important and legitimate interest in protecting the potentiality of human life. These interests are separate and distinct. Each grows in substantiality as the woman approaches term and, at a point during pregnancy, each becomes "compelling."

- *The Court is really trying to balance the rights of the state and the individual. Why?*

With respect to the State's important and legitimate interest in the health of the mother, the "compelling" point, in the light of present medical knowledge, is at approximately the end of the first trimester. This is so because of the now-established medical fact, that, until the end of the first trimester mortality in abortion may be less than mortality in normal childbirth. It follows that, from and after this point, a state may regulate the abortion procedure to the extent that the regulation reasonably relates to the preservation and protection of maternal health. Examples of permissible state regulation in this area are requirements as to the qualifications of the person who is to perform the abortion; as to the licensure of that person; as to the facility in which the procedure is to be performed, that is, whether it must be a hospital or may be a clinic or some other place of less-than-hospital status; as to the licensing of the facility; and the like.

This means, on the other hand, that, for the period of pregnancy prior to this "compelling" point, the attending physician, in consultation with his patient, is free to determine, without regulation by the state, that, in his medical judgment, the patient's pregnancy should be terminated. If that decision is reached, the judgment may be effectuated by an abortion free of interference by the state.

With respect to the state's important and legitimate interest in potential life, the "compelling" point is at viability. This is so because the fetus then presumably has the capability of meaningful life outside the mother's womb. State regulation protective of fetal life after viability thus has both logical and biological justifications. If the state is interested in protecting fetal life after viability, it may go so far as to proscribe abortion during that period, except when it is necessary to preserve the life or health of the mother.

Measured against these standards, the Texas Penal Code, in restricting legal abortions to those "procured or attempted by medical advice for the purpose of saving the life of the mother," sweeps too broadly. The statute makes no distinction between abortions performed early in pregnancy and those performed later, and it limits to a single reason, "saving" the mother's life, the legal justification for the procedure. The statute, therefore, cannot survive the constitutional attack made upon it here.

- *How does the Court ultimately balance the rights of the state versus the right of the individual? Do you think this is a fair balance? Why or why not?*

XI

To summarize and to repeat:

1. A state criminal abortion statute of the current Texas type, that excepts from criminality only a lifesaving procedure on behalf of the mother, without regard to pregnancy stage and without recognition of the other interests involved, is violative of the Due Process Clause of the Fourteenth Amendment.

(a) For the stage prior to approximately the end of the first trimester, the abortion decision and its effectuation must be left to the medical judgment of the pregnant woman's attending physician.

(b) For the stage subsequent to approximately the end of the first trimester, the state, in promoting its interest in the health of the mother, may, if it chooses, regulate the abortion procedure in ways that are reasonably related to maternal health.

(c) For the stage subsequent to viability, the state in promoting its interest in the potentiality of human life may, if it chooses, regulate, and even proscribe, abortion except where it is necessary, in appropriate medical judgment, for the preservation of the life or health of the mother.

2. The state may define the term "physician," as it has been employed in the preceding paragraphs of this Part XI of this opinion, to mean only a physician currently licensed by the state, and may proscribe any abortion by a person who is not a physician as so defined.

This holding, we feel, is consistent with the relative weights of the respective interests involved, with the lessons and examples of medical and legal history, with the lenity of the common law, and with the demands of the profound problems of the present day. The decision leaves the State free to place increasing restrictions on abortion as the period of pregnancy lengthens, so long as those restrictions are tailored to the recognized state interests. The decision vindicates the right of the physician to administer medical treatment according to his professional judgment up to the points where important state interests provide compelling justifications for intervention. Up to those points, the abortion decision in all its aspects is inherently, and primarily, a medical decision, and basic responsibility for it must rest with the physician. If an individual practitioner abuses the privilege of exercising proper medical judgment, the usual remedies, judicial and intra-professional, are available.

- *Why does the Court include a summary of their findings? What does that tell you about its decision?*

MR. JUSTICE REHNQUIST, dissenting.

The Court's opinion brings to the decision of this troubling question both extensive historical fact and a wealth of legal scholarship. While the opinion thus commands my respect, I find myself nonetheless in fundamental disagreement with those parts of it that invalidate the Texas statute in question, and therefore dissent.

I

The Court's opinion decides that a state may impose virtually no restriction on the performance of abortions during the first trimester of pregnancy. Our previous decisions indicate that a necessary predicate for such an opinion is a plaintiff who was in her first trimester of pregnancy at some time during the pendency of her lawsuit. While a party may vindicate his own constitutional rights, he may not seek vindication for the rights of others.

In deciding such a hypothetical lawsuit, the Court departs from the long-standing admonition that it should never "formulate a rule of constitutional law broader than is required by the precise facts to which it is to be applied."

II

Even if there were a plaintiff in this case capable of litigating the issue which the Court decides, I would reach a conclusion opposite to that reached by the Court. I have difficulty in concluding, as the Court does, that the right of "privacy" is involved in this case. Texas, by the statute here challenged, bars the performance of a medical abortion by a licensed physician on a plaintiff such as Roe. A transaction resulting in an operation such as this is not "private" in the ordinary usage of that word. Nor is the "privacy" that the Court finds here even a distant relative of the freedom from searches and seizures protected by the Fourth Amendment to the Constitution, which the Court has referred to as embodying a right to privacy.

If the Court means by the term "privacy" no more than that the claim of a person to be free from unwanted state regulation of consensual transactions may be a form of "liberty" protected by the Fourteenth Amendment, there is no doubt that similar claims have been upheld in our earlier decisions on the basis of that liberty. I agree with the statement of MR. JUSTICE STEWART in his concurring opinion that the "liberty," against deprivation of which without due process the Fourteenth Amendment protects, embraces more than the rights found in the Bill of Rights. But that liberty is not guaranteed absolutely against deprivation, only against deprivation without due process of law.

The Court eschews the history of the Fourteenth Amendment in its reliance on the "compelling state interest" test. See *Weber v. Aetna Casualty & Surety Co.* But the Court adds a new wrinkle to this test by transposing it from the legal considerations associated with the Equal Protection Clause of the Fourteenth Amendment to this case arising under the Due Process Clause of the Fourteenth Amendment. Unless I misapprehend the consequences of this transplanting of the "compelling state interest test," the Court's opinion will accomplish the seemingly impossible feat of leaving this area of the law more confused than it found it. While the Court's opinion quotes from the dissent of Mr. Justice Holmes in *Lochner v. New York*, the result it reaches is more closely attuned to the majority opinion of Mr. Justice Peckham in that case. As in *Lochner* and similar cases applying substantive due process standards to economic and social welfare legislation, the adoption of the compelling state interest standard will inevitably require this Court to examine the legislative policies and pass on the wisdom of these policies in the very process of deciding whether a particular state interest put forward may or may not be "compelling." The decision here to break pregnancy into three distinct terms and to outline the permissible restrictions the state may impose in each one, for example, partakes more of judicial legislation than it does of a determination of the intent of the drafters of the Fourteenth Amendment.

There apparently was no question concerning the validity of this provision or of any of the other state statutes when the Fourteenth Amendment was adopted. The only conclusion possible from this history is that the drafters did not intend to have the Fourteenth Amendment withdraw from the States the power to legislate with respect to this matter.

III

Even if one were to agree that the case that the Court decides were here, and that the enunciation of the substantive constitutional law in the Court's opinion were proper, the actual disposition of the case by the Court is still difficult to justify. The Texas statute is struck down *in toto*, even though the Court apparently concedes that, at later periods of pregnancy Texas might impose these self-same statutory limitations on abortion. My understanding of past practice is that a statute found to be invalid as applied to a particular plaintiff, but not unconstitutional as a whole, is not simply "struck down" but is, instead, declared unconstitutional as applied to the fact situation before the Court.

- *What are reasons that Justice Rehnquist disagrees with the majority?*

For all of the foregoing reasons, I respectfully dissent.

Connecting, Arguing, and Analyzing the Case

1. The two sides of *Roe v. Wade* (1973) still persist today. On one side is an individual's right to privacy"—a women's right to choices over her body. On the other side, is the state's "compelling interest" in regulating abortion—both for the safety and health of the mother and protecting the potentiality of the life of the unborn child. Discuss what the Court should consider in balancing these interests.
2. In part VI of the opinion, the Court discusses the positions of the American Medical Association, the American Public Health Association, and the American Bar Association. An amicus curiae brief is a written submission to the Court by a party not directly involved in the case but who believes there is important information that the Court should hear from them about the case to help the Court make its decision. Write your own amicus brief where you give your reasoning to support one of these organizations.

3. In 1996, the governor of Oklahoma, Mary Fallin, vetoed a bill that would have effectively banned abortion in the state by making the performance of the procedure a felony because she claimed it was constitutionally vague. The Court in *Roe v. Wade* (1973) dismissed the case of James Hubert Hallford, a licensed physician, who had previously been arrested for violations of the Texas abortion statues. But the Court did focus much of its opinion on the physician and his or her medical expertise and rights. The Court states, "The attending physician, in consultation with his patient, is free to determine, without regulation by the state, that, in his medical judgment, the patient's pregnancy should be terminated." Articulate a defensible claim, using relevant reasoning of the Court in *Roe v. Wade*, that the Oklahoma bill is not constitutionally vague.
4. Pennsylvania enacted several limitations to their abortion statue including requiring informed consent and a twenty-four-hour waiting period. A minor required the consent of one parent. A married woman had to notify her husband. A lawsuit was filed by Planned Parenthood alleging these restrictions violated a woman's right to receive an abortion as guaranteed by *Roe v. Wade* (1973). In the ensuing case, *Planned Parenthood of Southeastern Pennsylvania v. Casey* (1992), the Court set a new standard on laws imposing restrictions on abortion. The state's regulation may not place an "undue burden" on a woman's right to an abortion. An "undue burden" is one that puts a "substantial obstacle in the path of a woman seeking an abortion before the fetus attains viability." The Court upheld all of the provisions except spousal notification.

   a. Identify the constitutional right that is common to both *Roe v. Wade* (1973) and *Planned Parenthood of Southeastern Pennsylvania v. Casey* (1992).
   b. Based on the constitutional right identified in part a, explain how *Planned Parenthood of Southeastern Pennsylvania v. Casey* (1992) changed *Roe v. Wade* (1973).
   c. Compare the Court's reasoning in *Roe v. Wade* (1973) versus *Parenthood of Southeastern Pennsylvania v. Casey* (1992). Does the *Casey* decision limit or expand the right to an abortion? Explain.

Chapter Twelve

Shaw v. Reno

The Fifteenth Amendment, passed in 1870, states that the "right of citizens of the United States to vote shall not be denied or abridged by the United States or by any state on account of race, color, or previous condition of servitude," but discriminatory practices prevented this right from being realized for almost a century. The Voting Act of 1965 attempted to remove the obstacles that states had implemented to prevent African Americans from voting.

Some jurisdictions then looked for other ways to weaken the voting power of minorities, which led to racial gerrymandering, redistricting so that minorities were divided into different districts and therefore prevented from electing their choice for a candidate.

In 1962, the Court decided *Baker v. Carr*, which became a landmark case regarding redistricting as it made redistricting a justiciable issue. The Court articulated the "one person, one vote" formula. This decision cleared the way to challenge the apportionment of districts.

The Court in *Shaw v. Reno* decided that under the equal protections clause, redistricting must be examined under the standard strict scrutiny, which requires the redistricting to have a compelling government interest, be narrowly tailored to meet that goal, and be the least restrictive means for achieving that interest. The redistricting must also be conscious of race in order to comply with the Voting Act of 1965.

Legal Issue

Under the Fourteenth Amendment's Equal Protection Clause, did the North Carolina residents' claim that the state created a racially gerrymandered district raise a constitutionally valid issue?

Vocabulary

Propriety: the appropriateness
Reapportionment: to redivide
Gerrymandering: "to divide or arrange (a territorial unit) into election districts to give one political party an electoral majority in a large number of districts while concentrating the voting strength of the opposition in as few districts as possible" (Merriam-Webster)
Abridging: shortening
Pretextual: giving reasons for an act in order to hide the real reasons
Egregious: extremely bad
Diluted: to decrease the strength
Stigmatize: to mark with disapproval
Grandfather Clause: "a clause creating an exemption based on circumstances previously existing *especially* : a provision in several southern state constitutions designed to enfranchise poor whites and disenfranchise blacks by waiving high voting requirements for descendants of men voting before 1867" (Merriam-Webster)
Uncouth: "lacking in polish or grace" (Merriam-Webster)
Constituency: "the residents in an electoral district" (Merriam-Webster)

Parties in the Case

Petitioner: Five North Carolina residents
Respondent: Janet Reno, the attorney general, on behalf of the federal government
Edited version of case in the original language with distractors removed.

SHAW V. RENO, 509 U.S. 630 (1993)

JUSTICE O'CONNOR delivered the opinion of the Court.

This case involves two of the most complex and sensitive issues this Court has faced in recent years: the meaning of the constitutional "right" to vote, and the propriety of race-based state legislation designed to benefit members of historically disadvantaged racial minority groups. As a result of the 1990 census, North Carolina became entitled to a twelfth seat in the United States House of Representatives. The General Assembly enacted a reapportionment plan that included one majority-black congressional district. After the Attorney General of the United States objected to the plan pursuant to §5 of the Voting Rights Act of 1965, the General Assembly passed new legislation creating a second majority-black district. Appellants allege that the revised plan, which contains district boundary lines of dramatically irregular shape, constitutes an unconstitutional racial gerrymander. The question before us is whether appellants have stated a cognizable claim.

- *What is the latest legislation that the General Assembly passed in an attempt to comply with the Voting Rights Act?*

I

The voting age population of North Carolina is approximately 78 percent white, 20 percent black, and 1 percent Native American; the remaining 1 percent is predominantly Asian. The black population is relatively dispersed; blacks constitute a majority of the general population in only 5 of the State's 100 counties. Geographically, the State divides into three regions: the eastern Coastal Plain, the central Piedmont Plateau, and the western mountains. The General Assembly's first redistricting plan contained one majority-black district centered in that area of the State.

- *Make a visual of North Carolina outlining the information the Court gives in the paragraph above.*

Forty of North Carolina's one hundred counties are covered by §5 of the Voting Rights Act of 1965 which prohibits a jurisdiction subject to its provisions from implementing changes in a "standard, practice, or procedure with respect to voting" without federal authorization. The jurisdiction must obtain either a judgment from the United States District Court for the District of Columbia declaring that the proposed change "does not have the purpose and will not have the effect of denying or abridging the right to vote on account of race or color" or administrative preclearance from the Attorney General. Because the General Assembly's reapportionment plan affected the covered counties, the parties agree that §5 applied. The state chose to submit its plan to the Attorney General for preclearance.

- *What was the purpose behind the Voting Rights Act? What are the ways a jurisdiction subject to the Voting Rights Act can get changes approved?*

The Attorney General, acting through the Assistant Attorney General for the Civil Rights Division, interposed a formal objection to the General Assembly's plan. The Attorney General specifically objected to the configuration of boundary lines drawn in the south-central to southeastern region of the state. In the Attorney General's view, the General Assembly could have created a second majority-minority district "to give effect to black and Native American voting strength in this area" by using boundary lines "no more irregular than [those] found elsewhere in the proposed plan," but failed to do so for "pretextual reasons."

- *Why didn't the Attorney General approve the General Assembly's plan?*

Under §5, the state remained free to seek a declaratory judgment from the District Court for the District of Columbia notwithstanding the Attorney General's objection. It did not do so. Instead, the General Assembly enacted a revised redistricting plan that included a second majority-black district. The General Assembly located the second district not in the south-central to southeastern part of the State, but in the north-central region along Interstate 85.

The first of the two majority-black districts contained in the revised plan, District 1, is somewhat hook shaped. Centered in the northeast portion of the State, it moves southward until it tapers to a narrow band; then, with finger-like extensions, it reaches far into the southern-most part of the State near the South Carolina border. District 1 has been compared to a "Rorschach inkblot test."

The second majority-black district, District 12, is even more unusually shaped. It is approximately 160 miles long and, for much of its length, no wider than the I-85 corridor. It winds in snake like fashion through tobacco country, financial centers, and manufacturing areas "until it gobbles in enough enclaves of black neighborhoods." Of the 10 counties through which District 12 passes, 5 are cut into 3 different districts; even towns are divided. At one point, the district remains contiguous only because it intersects at a single point with two other districts before crossing over them.

- *Add this information to your visual.*

The Attorney General did not object to the General Assembly's revised plan. But numerous North Carolinians did. The North Carolina Republican Party and individual voters brought suit . . . alleging that the plan constituted an unconstitutional political gerrymander under *Davis v. Bandemer*.

- *Who is objecting to the revised plan (that is approved by the Attorney General)? Brainstorm why they would object to this plan.*

II

A

"The right to vote freely for the candidate of one's choice is of the essence of a democratic society. . . ." (*Reynolds v. Sims*). For much of our Nation's history, that right sadly has been denied to many because of race. The Fifteenth Amendment, ratified in 1870 after a bloody Civil War, promised unequivocally that "[t]he right of citizens of the United States to vote" no longer would be "denied or abridged . . . by any State on account of race, color, or previous condition of servitude."

But "[a] number of states . . . refused to take no for an answer and continued to circumvent the fifteenth amendment's prohibition through the use of both subtle and blunt instruments, perpetuating ugly patterns of pervasive racial discrimination." Ostensibly race-neutral devices such as literacy tests with "grandfather" clauses and "good character" provisos were devised to deprive black voters of the franchise. Another of the weapons in the States' arsenal was the racial gerrymander—"the deliberate and arbitrary distortion of district boundaries . . . for [racial] purposes."

- *How have states denied people of color from voting (despite the passing of the Fifteenth Amendment)?*

B

It is against this background that we confront the questions presented here. Our focus is on appellants' claim that the state engaged in unconstitutional racial gerrymandering. That argument strikes a powerful historical chord: it is unsettling how closely the North Carolina plan resembles the most egregious racial gerrymanders of the past.

- *Restate in your own words the Court's inquiry.*

An understanding of the nature of appellants' claim is critical to our resolution of the case. In their complaint, appellants did not claim that the General Assembly's reapportionment plan unconstitutionally "diluted" white voting strength. They did not even claim to be white. Rather, appellants' complaint alleged that the deliberate segregation of voters into separate districts on the basis of race violated their constitutional right to participate in a "colorblind" electoral process.

Despite their invocation of the ideal of a "color-blind" Constitution, appellants appear to concede that race-conscious redistricting is not always unconstitutional. That concession is wise: this Court never has held that race-conscious state decision making is impermissible in all circumstances. What appellants object to is redistricting legislation that is so extremely irregular on its face that it rationally can be viewed only as an effort to segregate the races for purposes of voting, without regard for traditional districting principles and without sufficiently compelling justification. For the reasons that follow, we conclude that appellants have stated a claim upon which relief can be granted under the Equal Protection Clause.

- *Restate the appellants' (the five North Carolina citizens) claim.*

III

A

The Equal Protection Clause provides that "[n]o State shall . . . deny to any person within its jurisdiction the equal protection of the laws." Its central purpose is to prevent the states from purposefully discriminating between individuals on the basis of race. Laws that explicitly distinguish between individuals on racial grounds fall within the core of that prohibition.

No inquiry into legislative purpose is necessary when the racial classification appears on the face of the statute.

Classifications of citizens solely on the basis of race "are by their very nature odious to a free people whose institutions are founded upon the doctrine of equality." They threaten to stigmatize individuals by reason of their membership in a racial group and to incite racial hostility. Accordingly, we have held that the Fourteenth Amendment requires state legislation that expressly distinguishes among citizens because of their race to be narrowly tailored to further a compelling governmental interest.

These principles apply not only to legislation that contains explicit racial distinctions, but also to those "rare" statutes that, although race neutral, are, on their face, "unexplainable on grounds other than race."

- *What is the standard when the Court determines if laws that distinguish individuals based on race or race-neutral laws that are "unexplainable on grounds other than race" are constitutional?*

B

Appellants contend that redistricting legislation that is so bizarre on its face that it is "unexplainable on grounds other than race" demands the same close scrutiny that we give other state laws that classify citizens by race. Our voting rights precedents support that conclusion.

In *Guinn v. United States*, the Court invalidated under the Fifteenth Amendment a statute that imposed a literacy requirement on voters but contained a "grandfather clause" applicable to individuals and their lineal descendants entitled to vote "on [or prior to] January 1, 1866." The determinative consideration for the Court was that the law, though ostensibly race neutral, on its face "embod[ied] no exercise of judgment and rest[ed] upon no discernible reason" other than to circumvent the prohibitions of the Fifteenth

Amendment. In other words, the statute was invalid because, on its face, it could not be explained on grounds other than race.

The Court applied the same reasoning to the "uncouth twenty-eight-sided" municipal boundary line at issue in *Gomillion*. Although the statute that redrew the city limits of Tuskegee was race neutral on its face, plaintiffs alleged that its effect was impermissibly to remove from the city virtually all black voters and no white voters. The Court reasoned:

> If these allegations upon a trial remained uncontradicted or unqualified, the conclusion would be irresistible, tantamount for all practical purposes to a mathematical demonstration, that the legislation is solely concerned with segregating white and colored voters by fencing Negro citizens out of town so as to deprive them of their preexisting municipal vote.

The majority resolved the case under the Fifteenth Amendment. *Gomillion* thus supports appellants' contention that district lines obviously drawn for the purpose of separating voters by race require careful scrutiny under the Equal Protection Clause regardless of the motivations underlying their adoption.

The difficulty of proof, of course, does not mean that a racial gerrymander, once established, should receive less scrutiny under the Equal Protection Clause than other state legislation classifying citizens by race. Moreover, it seems clear to us that proof sometimes will not be difficult at all. In some exceptional cases, a reapportionment plan may be so highly irregular that, on its face, it rationally cannot be understood as anything other than an effort to "segregat[e] . . . voters" on the basis of race. *Gomillion*, in which a tortured municipal boundary line was drawn to exclude black voters, was such a case. So, too, would be a case in which a state concentrated a dispersed minority population in a single district by disregarding traditional districting principles such as compactness, contiguity, and respect for political subdivisions. We emphasize that these criteria are important not because they are constitutionally required—they are not—but because they are objective factors that may serve to defeat a claim that a district has been gerrymandered on racial lines.

- *Summarize the precedent that the Court uses to justify its decision.*

Put differently, we believe that reapportionment is one area in which appearances do matter. A reapportionment plan that includes in one district individuals who belong to the same race, but who are otherwise widely separated by geographical and political boundaries, and who may have little in common with one another but the color of their skin, bears an uncomfortable resemblance to political apartheid. It reinforces the perception that members of the same racial group—regardless of their age, education, economic status, or the community in which they live—think alike, share the same political interests, and will prefer the same candidates at the polls. We have rejected such perceptions elsewhere as impermissible racial stereotypes.

The message that such districting sends to elected representatives is equally pernicious. When a district obviously is created solely to effectuate the perceived common interests of one racial group, elected officials are more likely to believe that their primary obligation is to represent only the members of that group, rather than their constituency as a whole. This is altogether antithetical to our system of representative democracy. As Justice Douglas explained in his dissent in *Wright v. Rockefeller* nearly 30 years ago:

> Here the individual is important, not his race, his creed, or his color. The principle of equality is at war with the notion that District A must be represented by a Negro, as it is with the notion that District B must be represented by a Caucasian, District C by a Jew, District D by a Catholic, and so on. . . . That system, by whatever name it is called, is a divisive force in a community, emphasizing differences between candidates and voters that are irrelevant in the constitutional sense. . . .

For these reasons, we conclude that a plaintiff challenging a reapportionment statute under the Equal Protection Clause may state a claim by alleging that the legislation, though race neutral on its face, rationally cannot be understood as anything other than an effort to separate voters into different districts on the basis of race, and that the separation lacks sufficient justification. It is unnecessary for us to decide whether or how a reapportionment plan that, on its face, can be explained in nonracial terms successfully could be challenged. Thus, we express no view as to whether "the intentional creation of majority-minority districts, without more," always gives rise to an equal protection claim. We hold only that, on the facts of this case, appellants have stated a claim sufficient to defeat the state appellees' motion to dismiss.

It is so ordered.

- *The Court decides that the redistricting under these facts was unconstitutional because it could not pass the standard of strict scrutiny. Under strict scrutiny, a law must be narrowly tailored, have a compelling government interest, and be the least restrictive means for achieving that interest. Describe the state's compelling government interest in their redistricting plan. Could it have been achieved a different way?*

JUSTICE WHITE, with whom JUSTICE BLACKMUN and JUSTICE STEVENS join, dissenting.

The facts of this case mirror those presented in *United Jewish Organizations of Williamsburgh, Inc. v. Carey*, where the Court rejected a claim that creation of a majority-minority district violated the Constitution, either as a per se matter or in light of the circumstances leading to the creation of such a district. Of particular relevance, five of the Justices reasoned that members of the white majority could not plausibly argue that their influence over the political process had been unfairly canceled, or that such had been the State's intent. Accordingly, they held that plaintiffs were not entitled to relief under the Constitution's Equal Protection Clause. On the same reasoning, I would affirm the District Court's dismissal of appellants' claim in this instance.

- *Summarize the decision in* United Jewish Organizations.

I

A

The grounds for my disagreement with the majority are simply stated: appellants have not presented a cognizable claim, because they have not alleged a cognizable injury. To date, we have held that only two types of state voting practices could give rise to a constitutional claim. The first involves direct and outright deprivation of the right to vote, for example by means of a poll tax or literacy test. The second type of unconstitutional practice is that which "affects the political strength of various groups," in violation of the Equal Protection Clause. As for this latter category, we have insisted that members of the political or racial group demonstrate that the challenged action have the intent and effect of unduly diminishing their influence on the political process. Although this severe burden has limited the number of successful suits, it was adopted for sound reasons.

- *In order to have a cognizable claim, one must have suffered an injury or harm; the dissent says that there was no harm here. What are the two types of state voting practices that could give rise to a constitutional claim?*

Redistricting plans also reflect group interests, and inevitably are conceived with partisan aims in mind. To allow judicial interference whenever this occurs would be to invite constant and unmanageable intrusion. Moreover, a group's power to affect the political process does not automatically dissipate by virtue of an electoral loss. Accordingly, we have asked that an identifiable group demonstrate more than mere lack of success at the polls to make out a successful gerrymandering claim.

With these considerations in mind, we have limited such claims by insisting upon a showing that "the political processes . . . were not equally open to participation by the group in question—that its members had less opportunity than did other residents in the district to participate in the political processes and to elect legislators of their choice."

I summed up my views on this matter in the plurality opinion in *Davis v. Bandemer*. Because districting inevitably is the expression of interest group politics, and because "the power to influence the political process is not limited to winning elections," the question in gerrymandering cases is "whether a particular group has been unconstitutionally denied its chance to effectively influence the political process." Thus, an equal protection violation may be found only where the electoral system substantially disadvantages certain voters in their opportunity to influence the political process effectively.

- Summarize the dissent's reasoning. When would one qualify for a cognizable injury based on a group's political strength being diminished?

Connecting, Arguing, and Analyzing the Case

1. The Court in *Reno v. Shaw* (1993) decided that redistricting must be examined under the standard of "strict scrutiny," which requires the redistricting to have a compelling government interest, be narrowly tailored to meet that goal, and be the least restrictive means for achieving that interest. The redistricting must also be conscious of race in order to comply with the Voting Act of 1965. Discuss how states maintain the balance of considering race but not violating the equal protections clause.
2. The dissenting opinions in *Reno v. Shaw* (1993) were concerned that the Equal Protections Clause was now being used to hurt a minority group. Explain the implications of applying strict scrutiny in a "colorblind" way.
3. What are politicians' goals when they gerrymander districts? Considering *Reno v. Shaw* (1993) and the previous case, *Baker v. Carr* (1962), what are the limitations the Court places on redistricting?
4. In *United Jewish Organization of Williamsburgh, Inc. v. Carey* (1977), the Court decided that white voters had not suffered any injury because they had not lost their political influence. In this case, the Court decided states could attempt to apportion districts so that racial minorities were not outvoted by white populations.

    a. Identify the constitutional clause that is common to both *United Jewish Organization of Williamsburgh, Inc. v. Carey* (1977) and *Shaw v. Reno* (1993).
    b. Based on the constitutional clause identified in part a, explain how the Court's decisions *United Jewish Organization of Willi-*

amsburgh, Inc. v. Carey (1977) and *Shaw v. Reno* (1993) are distinguished.

Chapter Thirteen

United States v. Lopez

The Commerce Clause allows Congress in Article I, Section 8, of the Constitution "[t]o make all Laws which shall be necessary and proper for carrying into Execution" its authority to "regulate Commerce with foreign Nations, and among the several States." Historically, the Supreme Court intervened with the actions of corporate entities in order to protect the consumer, whether it be to protect the marketplace or to protect the consumer from harmful substances. However, in recent years, the focus of the Court has expanded to examine whether actions taken by individuals in their own states violate the Commerce Clause by regulating activities and actions not specifically referred to in the Constitution.

Prosecuted under the Gun-Free School Zones Act of 1990, Alfonso Lopez Jr., a senior at Edison High School in San Antonio, Texas, was convicted of possessing a revolver that he intended to sell to another person. In a 5–4 decision, the Supreme Court in *United States v. Lopez* considered whether Congress had the right to legislate control over public schools and what can be done on their campuses under the Commerce Clause.

Legal Issue

Does Section 922(q) of the Gun-Free School Zones Act of 1990 exceed the power of Congress under the Commerce Clause?

Vocabulary

Commerce: the exchange or buying and selling of commodities on a large scale involving transportation from place to place
Intrastate: existing or occurring within a state

Interstate: of, connecting, or existing between two or more states especially of the United States
Intercourse: connection or dealings between persons or groups
Aggregate: taking all units as a whole
Rational basis: a reason or ground (as for legislation or an action by a government agency) that is not unreasonable or arbitrary and that bears a rational relationship to a legitimate state interest

Parties in the Case

Petitioner: U.S. government
Respondent: Alfonso Lopez Jr.
Edited version of case in the original language with distractors removed.

UNITED STATES V. LOPEZ, 514 U.S. 549 (1995)

CHIEF JUSTICE REHNQUIST delivered the opinion of the Court.

In the Gun-Free School Zones Act of 1990, Congress made it a federal offense "for any individual knowingly to possess a firearm at a place that the individual knows, or has reasonable cause to believe, is a school zone." The Act neither regulates a commercial activity nor contains a requirement that the possession be connected in any way to interstate commerce. We hold that the Act exceeds the authority of Congress "[t]o regulate Commerce . . . among the several States."

On March 10, 1992, respondent, who was then a 12th grade student, arrived at Edison High School in San Antonio, Texas, carrying a concealed .38 caliber handgun and five bullets. Acting upon an anonymous tip, school authorities confronted respondent, who admitted that he was carrying the weapon. He was arrested and charged under Texas law with firearm possession on school premises. The next day, the state charges were dismissed after federal agents charged respondent by complaint with violating the Gun-Free School Zones Act of 1990.

A federal grand jury indicted respondent on one count of knowing possession of a firearm at a school zone, in violation of § 922(q). Respondent moved to dismiss his federal indictment on the ground that § 922(q) "is unconstitutional as it is beyond the power of Congress to legislate control over our public schools." The District Court denied the motion, concluding that § 922(q) "is a constitutional exercise of Congress' well-defined power to regulate activities in and affecting commerce, and the 'business' of elementary, middle and high schools . . . affects interstate commerce." Respondent waived his right to a jury trial. The District Court conducted a bench trial, found him guilty of violating § 922(q), and sentenced him to six months' imprisonment and two years' supervised release.

- *How do schools have an effect on interstate commerce?*

On appeal, respondent challenged his conviction based on his claim that § 922(q) exceeded Congress' power to legislate under the Commerce Clause. The Court of Appeals for the Fifth Circuit agreed and reversed respondent's conviction. It held that, in light of what it characterized as insufficient congressional findings and legislative history, "section 922(q), in the full reach of its terms, is invalid as beyond the power of Congress under the Commerce Clause." Because of the importance of the issue, we granted certiorari, and we now affirm.

The Constitution delegates to Congress the power "[t]o regulate Commerce with foreign Nations, and among the several States, and with the Indian Tribes." Art. I, § 8, 1. 3. The Court, through Chief Justice Marshall, first defined the nature of Congress' commerce power in *Gibbons v. Ogden*:

> Commerce, undoubtedly, is traffic, but it is something more: it is intercourse. It describes the commercial intercourse between nations, and parts of nations, in all its branches, and is regulated by prescribing rules for carrying on that intercourse.

The commerce power "is the power to regulate; that is, to prescribe the rule by which commerce is to be governed. This power, like all others vested in congress, is complete in itself, may be exercised to its utmost extent, and acknowledges no limitations, other than are prescribed in the constitution."

For nearly a century thereafter, the Court's Commerce Clause decisions dealt but rarely with the extent of Congress' power, and almost entirely with the Commerce Clause as a limit on state legislation that discriminated against interstate commerce.

[W]e have identified three broad categories of activity that Congress may regulate under its commerce power. First, Congress may regulate the use of the channels of interstate commerce. Second, Congress is empowered to regulate and protect the instrumentalities of interstate commerce, or persons or things in interstate commerce, even though the threat may come only from intrastate activities. Finally, Congress' commerce authority includes the power to regulate those activities having a substantial relation to interstate commerce.

Within this final category, admittedly, our case law has not been clear whether an activity must "affect" or "substantially affect" interstate commerce in order to be within Congress' power to regulate it under the Commerce Clause. We conclude, consistent with the great weight of our case law, that the proper test requires an analysis of whether the regulated activity "substantially affects" interstate commerce.

We now turn to consider the power of Congress, in the light of this framework, to enact § 922(q). The first two categories of authority may be quickly disposed of: § 922(q) is not a regulation of the use of the channels of interstate commerce, nor is it an attempt to prohibit the interstate transportation of a commodity through the channels of commerce; nor can § 922(q) be justified as a regulation by which Congress has sought to protect an instrumentality of interstate commerce or a thing in interstate commerce. Thus, if § 922(q) is to be sustained, it must be under the third category as a regulation of an activity that substantially affects interstate commerce.

- *What is the difference between "affecting" and "substantially affecting" interstate commerce? Why do you think the Court thinks it's necessary to draw this distinction?*

First, we have upheld a wide variety of congressional Acts regulating intrastate economic activity where we have concluded that the activity substantially affected interstate commerce. . . . Where economic activity substantially affects interstate commerce, legislation regulating that activity will be sustained.

- *What are some examples of a state's attempt to regulate intrastate commerce that you think could have an impact in interstate commerce?*

Section 922(q) is a criminal statute that by its terms has nothing to do with "commerce" or any sort of economic enterprise, however broadly one might define those terms. Section 922(q) is not an essential part of a larger regulation of economic activity, in which the regulatory scheme could be undercut unless the intrastate activity were regulated. It cannot, therefore, be sustained under our cases upholding regulations of activities that arise out of or are connected with a commercial transaction, which viewed in the aggregate, substantially affects interstate commerce.

The government's essential contention, in fine, is that we may determine here that § 922(q) is valid because possession of a firearm in a local school zone does indeed substantially affect interstate commerce. The government argues that possession of a firearm in a school zone may result in violent crime and that violent crime can be expected to affect the functioning of the national economy in two ways. First, the costs of violent crime are substantial, and, through the mechanism of insurance, those costs are spread throughout the population. Second, violent crime reduces the willingness of individuals to travel to areas within the country that are perceived to be unsafe. The government also argues that the presence of guns in schools poses a substantial threat to the educational process by threatening the learning environment. A handicapped educational process, in turn, will result in a less productive citizenry. That, in turn, would have an adverse effect on the Nation's economic well-being. As a result, the government argues that Congress could rationally have concluded that § 922(q) substantially affects interstate commerce.

- *The Court points out that the statute under consideration is actually a criminal statute beyond the reach of the Commerce Clause. The government says there is a connection between school safety and interstate commerce. Which argument do you find more compelling? This case was decided before the first high-profile school shooting case in Littleton, Colorado, in 1999. Do you think that if this case were considered today, the Court should take the rise in school shootings into consideration?*

We pause to consider the implications of the government's arguments. The government admits, under its "costs of crime" reasoning, that Congress could regulate not only all violent crime, but all activities that might lead to violent crime, regardless of how tenuously they relate to interstate commerce. Similarly, under the Government's "national productivity" reasoning, Congress could regulate any activity that it found was related to the economic productivity of individual citizens: family law (including marriage, divorce, and child custody), for example. Under the theories that the government presents in support of § 922(q), it is difficult to perceive any limitation on federal power, even in areas such as criminal law enforcement or education where states historically have been sovereign. Thus, if we were to accept the government's arguments, we are hard pressed to posit any activity by an individual that Congress is without power to regulate.

- *Essentially, the Court says if it allowed the Commerce Clause to be used to regulate guns in schools, it could justify any law using the Commerce Clause. Do you agree with this argument? How do you think it could be extrapolated to the family law issues the Court mentions?*

Although JUSTICE BREYER argues that acceptance of the Government's rationales would not authorize a general federal police power, he is unable to identify any activity that the states may regulate but Congress may not. JUSTICE BREYER posits that there might be some limitations on Congress' commerce power, such as family law or certain aspects of education. These suggested limitations, when viewed in light of the dissent's expansive analysis, are devoid of substance.

JUSTICE BREYER focuses, for the most part, on the threat that firearm possession in and near schools poses to the educational process and the potential economic consequences flowing from that threat. Specifically, the dissent reasons that (1) gun-related violence is a serious problem; (2) that problem, in turn, has an adverse effect on classroom learning; and (3) that adverse effect on classroom learning, in turn, represents a substantial threat to trade and commerce. This analysis would be equally applicable, if not more so, to subjects such as family law and direct regulation of education.

For instance, if Congress can, pursuant to its Commerce Clause power, regulate activities that adversely affect the learning environment, then, a fortiori, it also can regulate the educational process directly. Congress could determine that a school's curriculum has a "significant" effect on the extent of classroom learning. As a result, Congress could mandate a federal curriculum for local elementary and secondary schools because what is taught in local schools has a significant "effect on classroom learning," and that, in turn, has a substantial effect on interstate commerce.

JUSTICE BREYER rejects our reading of precedent and argues that "Congress . . . could rationally conclude that schools fall on the commercial side of the line." Again, JUSTICE BREYER'S rationale lacks any real limits because, depending on the level of generality, any activity can be looked upon as commercial. Under the dissent's rationale, Congress could just as easily look at child rearing as "fall[ing] on the commercial side of the line" because it provides a "valuable service—namely, to equip [children] with the skills they need to survive in life and, more specifically, in the workplace." We do not doubt that Congress has authority under the Commerce Clause to regulate numerous commercial activities that substantially affect interstate commerce and also affect the educational process. That authority, though broad, does not include the authority to regulate each and every aspect of local schools.

- *In Justice Breyer's dissent, he writes about the economic effect of education on the United States and that it is necessary to make schools safe to make the United States globally competitive. In his dissent, he argues that gun violence is a serious economic threat because the more violent a school is, the worse the education is, and then the less competitive the students are in the global market. Do you agree with this argument?*

Admittedly, a determination whether an intrastate activity is commercial or noncommercial may in some cases result in legal uncertainty. But, so long as Congress' authority is limited to those powers enumerated in the Constitution, and so long as those enumerated powers are interpreted as having judicially enforceable outer limits, congressional legislation under the Commerce Clause always will engender "legal uncertainty." As Chief Justice Marshall stated in *McCulloch v. Maryland*:

"Th[e] [federal] government is acknowledged by all to be one of enumerated powers. The principle, that it can exercise only the powers granted to it . . . is now universally admitted. But the question respecting the extent of the powers actually granted, is perpetually arising, and will probably continue to arise, as long as our system shall exist."

The Constitution mandates this uncertainty by withholding from Congress a plenary police power that would authorize enactment of every type of legislation. Congress has operated within this framework of legal uncertainty ever since this Court determined that it was the Judiciary's duty "to say what the law is." Any possible benefit from eliminating this "legal uncertainty" would be at the expense of the Constitution's system of enumerated powers.

- *Which Supreme Court case gave the judiciary the right to "say what the law is"?*

These are not precise formulations, and in the nature of things they cannot be. But we think they point the way to a correct decision of this case. The possession of a gun in a local school zone is in no sense an economic activity that might, through repetition elsewhere, substantially affect any sort of interstate commerce. Respondent was a local student at a local school; there is no indication that he had recently moved in interstate commerce, and there is no requirement that his possession of the firearm have any concrete tie to interstate commerce.

To uphold the government's contentions here, we would have to pile inference upon inference in a manner that would bid fair to convert congressional authority under the Commerce Clause to a general police power of the sort retained by the States. Admittedly, some of our prior cases have taken long steps down that road, giving great deference to congressional action. The broad language in these opinions has suggested the possibility of additional expansion, but we decline here to proceed any further. To do so would require us to conclude that the Constitution's enumeration of powers does not presuppose something not enumerated, and that there never will be a distinction between what is truly national and what is truly local. This we are unwilling to do.

For the foregoing reasons the judgment of the Court of Appeals is Affirmed.

Connecting, Arguing, and Analyzing the Case

1. Justice Rehnquist states in *Lopez* the three broad areas Congress has the power to control under the Commerce Clause. They are:

    a. the channels of interstate commerce;
    b. the instrumentalities of interstate commerce, or persons or things in interstate commerce;

c. activities that substantially affect or substantially relate to interstate commerce.

2. Using this rationale, do you think Congress could pass federal laws on the following activities and not violate the Commerce Clause? Explain why or why not.

   - car jacking
   - human trafficking
   - compulsory education
   - road taxes
   - minimum legal age to get married

3. How could Congress use its other powers to curb some of the "bad acts" they wish to control without creating laws that could potentially violate the Commerce Cause?
4. James Madison, the leading Federalist at the Constitutional Convention, wanted Congress to have limited power over commerce. What do you think he would say about recent Commerce Clause decisions by the Supreme Court in the past fifty years? Would he agree or disagree with them? Research Madison's opinion on the commerce clause and write an editorial to a newspaper that articulates his stance on what the Supreme Court should be saying in these cases.
5. Compare the holding in this case to the decisions in *Heart of Atlanta Motel, Inc. v. United States*, 379 U.S. 241 (1964) and *Gonzales v. Raich*, 545 U. S. 1 (2005). How are those cases different from the *Lopez* case?

Chapter Fourteen

Citizens United v. Federal Election Commission

Since the Industrial Revolution, Americans have been concerned about the involvement of corporations and the money coming from corporations as political influencers. From 1910 onward, Congress sought to pass laws that would prevent large corporate contributions from influencing elections. The Federal Elections Campaign Acts (FECA) of 1971 and 1974 strengthened campaign finance reporting and requirements, and it provided specific limits for contributions to political campaigns.

In *Buckley v. Valeo* (1976), portions of the FECA were struck down by the Supreme Court. The Court found that restricting independent spending by individuals and groups to support or defeat a candidate interfered with the First Amendment right of free speech, as long as those funds were spent independently and not from a candidate or a political campaign. After *Buckley*, there was a dramatic increase in political spending by political action committees (PACs), and Congress addressed this PAC spending by passing the Bipartisan Campaign Finance Reform Act (BCRA) in 2002. Part of the BRCA legislation prohibited electioneering communications, "speech naming a federal candidate within 30 days of a primary election or 60 days of a general election." Citizens United, a nonprofit financed by mostly individual donations with some for-profit donations, wanted to distribute and air a documentary about Senator Hillary Clinton before the 2008 primary election. Citizens United sought injunctive relief to prevent the federal laws from stopping them from showing the documentary in the days leading up to the election.

Legal Issue

Do laws preventing corporations and unions from using their general treasury funds for independent "electioneering communications" (political advertising) violate the First Amendment's guarantee of free speech?

Vocabulary

Stare decisis: following rules or principles laid down in previous judicial decisions unless they contravene the ordinary principles of justice
Declaratory relief: A judge's determination of the parties' rights under a statute. The theory is that an early resolution of legal rights will resolve some or all of the other issues in the matter.
Injunctive relief: a court-ordered act or prohibition against an act or condition that has been requested
Strict scrutiny: A form of judicial review that courts use to determine the constitutionality of certain laws. To pass strict scrutiny, the legislature must have passed the law to further a "compelling governmental interest" and must have narrowly tailored the law to achieve that interest.
Compelling interest: an essential or necessary governmental interest, rather than a matter of choice, preference, or discretion.
Antidistortion: preventing something from being distorted by the use of wealth beyond the real level of interest by the public
Anticorruption: opposing, discouraging, or punishing corruption
Quid pro quo: a favor or advantage granted or expected in return for something
Express advocacy: political advertisements that expressly and clearly support or oppose a particular electoral outcome

Parties in the Case

Petitioner: Citizens United, a nonprofit corporation
Respondent: The Federal Election Commission
   Edited version of case in the original language with distractors removed

CITIZENS UNITED V. FEDERAL ELECTION COMMISSION, 558 U.S. 310 (2010)

Justice Kennedy delivered the opinion of the Court.

Federal law prohibits corporations and unions from using their general treasury funds to make independent expenditures for speech defined as an "electioneering communication" or for speech expressly advocating the election or defeat of a candidate. 2 U.S.C.§441b. Limits on electioneering communications were upheld in *McConnell v. Federal Election Comm'n, 540 U.*

S. 93, 203–209 (2003). The holding of *McConnell* rested to a large extent on an earlier case, *Austin v. Michigan Chamber of Commerce,* 494 U. S. 652 (1990). *Austin* had held that political speech may be banned based on the speaker's corporate identity.

In this case we are asked to reconsider *Austin* and, in effect, *McConnell*. It has been noted that "Austin was a significant departure from ancient First Amendment principles." We agree with that conclusion and hold that stare decisis does not compel the continued acceptance of *Austin*. The government may regulate corporate political speech through disclaimer and disclosure requirements, but it may not suppress that speech altogether. We turn to the case now before us.

I

A

Citizens United is a nonprofit corporation. Citizens United has an annual budget of about $12 million. Most of its funds are from donations by individuals; but, in addition, it accepts a small portion of its funds from for-profit corporations.

In January 2008, Citizens United released a film entitled *Hillary: The Movie.* We refer to the film as *Hillary.* It is a 90-minute documentary about then-Senator Hillary Clinton, who was a candidate in the Democratic Party's 2008 presidential primary elections. *Hillary* mentions Senator Clinton by name and depicts interviews with political commentators and other persons, most of them quite critical of Senator Clinton. *Hillary* was released in theaters and on DVD, but Citizens United wanted to increase distribution by making it available through video-on-demand.

Video-on-demand allows digital cable subscribers to select programming from various menus, including movies, television shows, sports, news, and music. The viewer can watch the program at any time and can elect to rewind or pause the program. In December 2007, a cable company offered, for a payment of $1.2 million, to make *Hillary* available on a video-on-demand channel called "Elections '08." Some video-on-demand services require viewers to pay a small fee to view a selected program, but here the proposal was to make *Hillary* available to viewers free of charge.

To implement the proposal, Citizens United was prepared to pay for the video-on-demand; and to promote the film, it produced two 10-second ads and one 30-second ad for *Hillary.* Each ad includes a short (and, in our view, pejorative) statement about Senator Clinton, followed by the name of the movie and the movie's Website address. Citizens United desired to promote the video-on-demand offering by running advertisements on broadcast and cable television.

- Based on the information you've had in the case thus far, do you think the documentary in question would be sympathetic or critical of Hillary Clinton?

B

Before the Bipartisan Campaign Reform Act of 2002 (BCRA), federal law prohibited—and still does prohibit—corporations and unions from using general treasury funds to make direct contributions to candidates or independent expenditures that expressly advocate the election or defeat of a candidate, through any form of media, in connection with certain qualified federal elections. An electioneering communication is defined as "any broadcast, cable, or satellite communication" that "refers to a clearly identified candidate for Federal office" and is made within 30 days of a primary or 60 days of a general election. The Federal Election Commission's (FEC) regulations further define an electioneering communication as a communication that is "publicly distributed." "In the case of a candidate for nomination for President . . . publicly distributed means" that the communication "[c]an be received by 50,000 or more persons in a State where a primary election . . . is being held within 30 days." Corporations and unions are barred from using their general treasury funds for express advocacy or electioneering communications. They may establish, however, a "separate segregated fund" (known as a political action committee, or PAC) for these purposes. The moneys received by the segregated fund are limited to donations from stockholders and employees of the corporation or, in the case of unions, members of the union.

C

Citizens United wanted to make *Hillary* available through video-on-demand within 30 days of the 2008 primary elections. It feared, however, that both the film and the ads would be covered by §441b's ban on corporate-funded independent expenditures, thus subjecting the corporation to civil and criminal penalties. In December 2007, Citizens United sought declaratory and injunctive relief against the FEC. It argued that (1) §441b is unconstitutional as applied to *Hillary*; and (2) BCRA's disclaimer and disclosure requirements are unconstitutional as applied to *Hillary* and to the three ads for the movie.

The District Court denied Citizens United's motion for a preliminary injunction, 530 F. Supp. 2d 274 (DC 2008) (per curiam), and then granted the FEC's motion for summary judgment. The court held that §441b was facially constitutional under *McConnell*, and that §441b was constitutional as applied to *Hillary* because it was "susceptible of no other interpretation than to inform the electorate that Senator Clinton is unfit for office, that the United

States would be a dangerous place in a President Hillary Clinton world, and that viewers should vote against her." The court also rejected Citizens United's challenge to BCRA's disclaimer and disclosure requirements. It noted that "the Supreme Court has written approvingly of disclosure provisions triggered by political speech even though the speech itself was constitutionally protected under the First Amendment."

We noted probable jurisdiction. The case was reargued in this Court after the Court asked the parties to file supplemental briefs addressing whether we should overrule either or both *Austin* and the part of *McConnell* which addresses the facial validity of 2 U. S. C. §441b.

II

Before considering whether *Austin* should be overruled, we first address whether Citizens United's claim that §441b cannot be applied to *Hillary* may be resolved on other, narrower grounds.

The Court cannot resolve this case on a narrower ground without chilling political speech, speech that is central to the meaning and purpose of the First Amendment. It is not judicial restraint to accept an unsound, narrow argument just so the Court can avoid another argument with broader implications. Indeed, a court would be remiss in performing its duties were it to accept an unsound principle merely to avoid the necessity of making a broader ruling. Here, the lack of a valid basis for an alternative ruling requires full consideration of the continuing effect of the speech suppression upheld in Austin.

Citizens United stipulated to dismissing count 5 of its complaint, which raised a facial challenge to §441b, even though count 3 raised an as-applied challenge. See App. 23a (count 3: "As applied to *Hillary*, [§441b] is unconstitutional under the First Amendment guarantees of free expression and association"). The Government argues that Citizens United waived its challenge to *Austin* by dismissing count 5. We disagree.

The ongoing chill upon speech that is beyond all doubt protected makes it necessary in this case to invoke the earlier precedents that a statute which chills speech can and must be invalidated where its facial invalidity has been demonstrated. For these reasons we find it necessary to reconsider *Austin*.

III

The First Amendment provides that "Congress shall make no law . . . abridging the freedom of speech." Laws enacted to control or suppress speech may operate at different points in the speech process.

The law before us is an outright ban, backed by criminal sanctions. Section 441b makes it a felony for all corporations—including nonprofit advocacy corporations—either to expressly advocate the election or defeat of candidates or to broadcast electioneering communications within 30 days of a primary election and 60 days of a general election. Thus, the following acts would all be felonies under §441b: The Sierra Club runs an ad, within the crucial phase of 60 days before the general election, that exhorts the public to disapprove of a Congressman who favors logging in national forests; the National Rifle Association publishes a book urging the public to vote for the challenger because the incumbent U. S. Senator supports a handgun ban; and the American Civil Liberties Union creates a Web site telling the public to vote for a presidential candidate in light of that candidate's defense of free speech. These prohibitions are classic examples of censorship.

- *Why do you think Congress has regulated this type of speech from corporations? What is this statute trying to accomplish?*

Section 441b is a ban on corporate speech notwithstanding the fact that a PAC created by a corporation can still speak. A PAC is a separate association from the corporation. So the PAC exemption from §441b's expenditure ban, §441b(b)(2), does not allow corporations to speak. Even if a PAC could somehow allow a corporation to speak—and it does not—the option to form PACs does not alleviate the First Amendment problems with §441b. PACs are burdensome alternatives; they are expensive to administer and subject to extensive regulations. For example, every PAC must appoint a treasurer, forward donations to the treasurer promptly, keep detailed records of the identities of the persons making donations, preserve receipts for three years, and file an organization statement and report changes to this information within 10 days.

And that is just the beginning. PACs must file detailed monthly reports with the FEC, which are due at different times depending on the type of election that is about to occur:

> These reports must contain information regarding the amount of cash on hand; the total amount of receipts, detailed by 10 different categories; the identification of each political committee and candidate's authorized or affiliated committee making contributions, and any persons making loans, providing rebates, refunds, dividends, or interest or any other offset to operating expenditures in an aggregate amount over $200; the total amount of all disbursements, detailed by 12 different categories; the names of all authorized or affiliated committees to whom expenditures aggregating over $200 have been made; persons to whom loan repayments or refunds have been made; the total sum of all contributions, operating expenses, outstanding debts and obligations, and the settlement terms of the retirement of any debt or obligation.

- *Why do you think political action committees are subject to such stringent regulations?*

PACs have to comply with these regulations just to speak. This might explain why fewer than 2,000 of the millions of corporations in this country have PACs. PACs, furthermore, must exist before they can speak. Given the onerous restrictions, a corporation may not be able to establish a PAC in time to make its views known regarding candidates and issues in a current campaign.

Section 441b's prohibition on corporate independent expenditures is thus a ban on speech. As a "restriction on the amount of money a person or group can spend on political communication during a campaign," that statute "necessarily reduces the quantity of expression by restricting the number of issues discussed, the depth of their exploration, and the size of the audience reached." Were the Court to uphold these restrictions, the government could repress speech by silencing certain voices at any of the various points in the speech process. If §441b applied to individuals, no one would believe that it is merely a time, place, or manner restriction on speech. Its purpose and effect are to silence entities whose voices the government deems to be suspect.

Speech is an essential mechanism of democracy, for it is the means to hold officials accountable to the people. The right of citizens to inquire, to hear, to speak, and to use information to reach consensus is a precondition to enlightened self-government and a necessary means to protect it. The First Amendment "'has its fullest and most urgent application' to speech uttered during a campaign for political office."

For these reasons, political speech must prevail against laws that would suppress it, whether by design or inadvertence. Laws that burden political speech are "subject to strict scrutiny," which requires the government to prove that the restriction "furthers a compelling interest and is narrowly tailored to achieve that interest."

The Court has upheld a narrow class of speech restrictions that operate to the disadvantage of certain persons, but these rulings were based on an interest in allowing governmental entities to perform their functions. The corporate independent expenditures at issue in this case, however, would not interfere with governmental functions, so these cases are inapposite. These precedents stand only for the proposition that there are certain governmental functions that cannot operate without some restrictions on particular kinds of speech. By contrast, it is inherent in the nature of the political process that voters must be free to obtain information from diverse sources in order to determine how to cast their votes. At least before *Austin*, the Court had not allowed the exclusion of a class of speakers from the general public dialogue.

- *How does the Court distinguish between other speech restrictions it has allowed and the decision not to allow restrictions in political speech under the First Amendment?*

We find no basis for the proposition that, in the context of political speech, the government may impose restrictions on certain disfavored speakers. Both history and logic lead us to this conclusion.

A

1 The Court has recognized that First Amendment protection extends to corporations.

This protection has been extended by explicit holdings to the context of political speech. The Court has thus rejected the argument that political speech of corporations or other associations should be treated differently under the First Amendment simply because such associations are not "natural persons."

2 *Bellotti*, 435 U.S. 765, reaffirmed the First Amendment principle that the Government cannot restrict political speech based on the speaker's corporate identity. *Bellotti* could not have been clearer when it struck down a state-law prohibition on corporate independent expenditures related to referenda issues:

"We thus find no support in the First . . . Amendment, or in the decisions of this Court, for the proposition that speech that otherwise would be within the protection of the First Amendment loses that protection simply because its source is a corporation that cannot prove, to the satisfaction of a court, a material effect on its business or property. . . . [That proposition] amounts to an impermissible legislative prohibition of speech based on the identity of the interests that spokesmen may represent in public debate over controversial issues and a requirement that the speaker have a sufficiently great interest in the subject to justify communication.

"In the realm of protected speech, the legislature is constitutionally disqualified from dictating the subjects about which persons may speak and the speakers who may address a public issue."

It is important to note that the reasoning and holding of *Bellotti* did not rest on the existence of a viewpoint-discriminatory statute. It rested on the principle that the Government lacks the power to ban corporations from speaking.

3 Thus the law stood until *Austin*. *Austin* "uph[eld] a direct restriction on the independent expenditure of funds for political speech for the first time in [this Court's] history." There, the Michigan Chamber of Commerce sought to use general treasury funds to run a newspaper ad supporting a specific candidate. Michigan law, however, prohibited corporate independent expenditures that supported or opposed any candidate for state office. A violation of the law was punishable as a felony. The Court sustained the speech prohibition.

[T]he *Austin* Court identified a new governmental interest in limiting political speech: an antidistortion interest. *Austin* found a compelling governmental interest in preventing "the corrosive and distorting effects of immense aggregations of wealth that are accumulated with the help of the corporate form and that have little or no correlation to the public's support for the corporation's political ideas."

- *In what ways could you imagine that a corporation could distort the public support on an issue by using corporate wealth? How is this different from how individuals conduct political speech?*

B

The Court is thus confronted with conflicting lines of precedent: a pre-*Austin* line that forbids restrictions on political speech based on the speaker's corporate identity and a post-*Austin* line that permits them. No case before Austin had held that Congress could prohibit independent expenditures for political speech based on the speaker's corporate identity. Before *Austin* Congress had enacted legislation for this purpose, and the government urged the same proposition before this Court.

In its defense of the corporate-speech restrictions in §441b, the government notes the antidistortion rationale on which *Austin* and its progeny rest in part, yet it all but abandons reliance upon it. It argues instead that two other compelling interests support Austin's holding that corporate expenditure restrictions are constitutional: an anticorruption interest, see 494 U. S., at 678 (Stevens, J., concurring), and a shareholder-protection interest, see id., at 674–675 (Brennan, J., concurring). We consider the three points in turn.

1 As for *Austin's* antidistortion rationale, the Government does little to defend it. And with good reason, for the rationale cannot support §441b.

If the First Amendment has any force, it prohibits Congress from fining or jailing citizens, or associations of citizens, for simply engaging in political speech. If the antidistortion rationale were to be accepted, however, it would permit Government to ban political speech simply because the speaker is an association that has taken on the corporate form. The Government contends that *Austin* permits it to ban corporate expenditures for almost all forms of communication stemming from a corporation. If *Austin* were correct, the Government could prohibit a corporation from expressing political views in media beyond those presented here, such as by printing books. This troubling assertion of brooding governmental power cannot be reconciled with the confidence and stability in civic discourse that the First Amendment must secure.

Political speech is "indispensable to decision making in a democracy, and this is no less true because the speech comes from a corporation rather than an individual." This protection for speech is inconsistent with *Austin*'s antidistortion rationale. *Austin* sought to defend the antidistortion rationale as a means to prevent corporations from obtaining "'an unfair advantage in the political marketplace'" by using "'resources amassed in the economic marketplace.'"

Either as support for its antidistortion rationale or as a further argument, the *Austin* majority undertook to distinguish wealthy individuals from corporations on the ground that "[s]tate law grants corporations special advantages—such as limited liability, perpetual life, and favorable treatment of the accumulation and distribution of assets." This does not suffice, however, to allow laws prohibiting speech.

It is irrelevant for purposes of the First Amendment that corporate funds may "have little or no correlation to the public's support for the corporation's political ideas." All speakers, including individuals and the media, use money amassed from the economic marketplace to fund their speech. The First Amendment protects the resulting speech, even if it was enabled by economic transactions with persons or entities who disagree with the speaker's ideas.

Austin's antidistortion rationale would produce the dangerous, and unacceptable, consequence that Congress could ban political speech of media corporations. Media corporations are now exempt from §441b's ban on corporate expenditures. Yet media corporations accumulate wealth with the help of the corporate form, the largest media corporations have "immense aggregations of wealth," and the views expressed by media corporations often "have little or no correlation to the public's support" for those views. Thus, under the Government's reasoning, wealthy media corporations could have their voices diminished to put them on par with other media entities. There is no precedent for permitting this under the First Amendment.

- *Consider the political speech of CNN and Fox News. Should media entities be held to the same ban on political speech as put forth under Austin? Why or why not?*

The media exemption discloses further difficulties with the law now under consideration. There is no precedent supporting laws that attempt to distinguish between corporations which are deemed to be exempt as media corporations and those which are not. "We have consistently rejected the proposition that the institutional press has any constitutional privilege beyond that of other speakers." With the advent of the Internet and the decline of print and broadcast media, moreover, the line between the media and others who wish to comment on political and social issues becomes far more blurred.

- *Should media speech and corporate speech be seen differently?*

The law's exception for media corporations is, on its own terms, all but an admission of the invalidity of the antidistortion rationale. And the exemption results in a further, separate reason for finding this law invalid: Again by its own terms, the law exempts some corporations but covers others, even though both have the need or the motive to communicate their views. The exemption applies to media corporations owned or controlled by corporations that have diverse and substantial investments and participate in endeavors other than news. So even assuming the most doubtful proposition that a news organization has a right to speak when others do not, the exemption would allow a conglomerate that owns both a media business and an unrelated business to influence or control the media in order to advance its overall business interest. At the same time, some other corporation, with an identical business interest but no media outlet in its ownership structure, would be forbidden to speak or inform the public about the same issue. This differential treatment cannot be squared with the First Amendment.

There is simply no support for the view that the First Amendment, as originally understood, would permit the suppression of political speech by media corporations. The Framers may not have anticipated modern business and media corporations. Yet television networks and major newspapers owned by media corporations have become the most important means of mass communication in modern times. The First Amendment was certainly not understood to condone the suppression of political speech in society's most salient media. It was understood as a response to the repression of speech and the press that had existed in England and the heavy taxes on the press that were imposed in the colonies. The great debates between the Federalists and the Anti-Federalists over our founding document were published and expressed in the most important means of mass communication of that era—newspapers owned by individuals. At the founding, speech was open, comprehensive, and vital to society's definition of itself; there were no limits on the sources of speech and knowledge. The framers may have been unaware of certain types of speakers or forms of communication, but that does not mean that those speakers and media are entitled to less First Amendment protection than those types of speakers and media that provided the means of communicating political ideas when the Bill of Rights was adopted.

- *With the advent of different types of media, including social media, are Americans today getting the same access to political debates as they did during the time of the constitutional framers? What is better or worse about media exposure and access today?*

Austin interferes with the "open marketplace" of ideas protected by the First Amendment. It permits the government to ban the political speech of millions of associations of citizens. Most of these are small corporations without large amounts of wealth. This fact belies the government's argument that the statute is justified on the ground that it prevents the "distorting effects of immense aggregations of wealth." It is not even aimed at amassed wealth.

- *But should the government be concerned with the political speech of corporations with a large amount of wealth? Why or why not?*

The censorship we now confront is vast in its reach. The government has "muffle[d] the voices that best represent the most significant segments of the economy." And "the electorate [has been] deprived of information, knowledge and opinion vital to its function." By suppressing the speech of manifold corporations, both for-profit and nonprofit, the Government prevents their voices and viewpoints from reaching the public and advising voters on which persons or entities are hostile to their interests. Factions will necessarily form in our Republic, but the remedy of "destroying the liberty" of some factions is "worse than the disease." Factions should be checked by permitting them all to speak, and by entrusting the people to judge what is true and what is false.

- *Do you agree with the Court's point in the previous paragraph? Why or why not?*

The purpose and effect of this law is to prevent corporations, including small and nonprofit corporations, from presenting both facts and opinions to the public. This makes *Austin's* antidistortion rationale all the more an aberration. [S]maller or nonprofit corporations cannot raise a voice to object when other corporations, including those with vast wealth, are cooperating with the government. That cooperation may sometimes be voluntary, or it may be at the demand of a government official who uses his or her authority, influence, and power to threaten corporations to support the government's policies. Those kinds of interactions are often unknown and unseen. The speech that §441b forbids, though, is public, and all can judge its content and purpose. References to massive corporate treasuries should not mask the real operation of this law. Rhetoric ought not obscure reality.

- *Do you think the intent of §441b was to silence the political speech of small corporations?*

Even if §441b's expenditure ban were constitutional, wealthy corporations could still lobby elected officials, although smaller corporations may not have the resources to do so. And wealthy individuals and unincorporated associations can spend unlimited amounts on independent expenditures. Yet certain disfavored associations of citizens—those that have taken on the corporate form—are penalized for engaging in the same political speech.

- *What is your reaction to the Court's premise that large corporations could get around §441b anyway?*

When Government seeks to use its full power, including the criminal law, to command where a person may get his or her information or what distrusted source he or she may not hear, it uses censorship to control thought. This is unlawful. The First Amendment confirms the freedom to think for ourselves.

2   What we have said also shows the invalidity of other arguments made by the Government. For the most part relinquishing the antidistortion rationale, the Government falls back on the argument that corporate political speech can be banned in order to prevent corruption or its appearance.

With regard to large direct contributions, [the Court in *Buckley v. Valeo*, 424 U.S. 1 (1976)] reasoned that they could be given "to secure a political quid pro quo," and that "the scope of such pernicious practices can never be reliably ascertained." The practices Buckley noted would be covered by bribery laws if a quid pro quo arrangement were proved.

When *Buckley* identified a sufficiently important governmental interest in preventing corruption or the appearance of corruption, that interest was limited to quid pro quo corruption. The fact that speakers may have influence over or access to elected officials does not mean that these officials are corrupt:

"Favoritism and influence are not . . . avoidable in representative politics. It is in the nature of an elected representative to favor certain policies, and, by necessary corollary, to favor the voters and contributors who support those policies. It is well understood that a substantial and legitimate reason, if not the only reason, to cast a vote for, or to make a contribution to, one candidate over another is that the candidate will respond by producing those political outcomes the supporter favors. Democracy is premised on responsiveness."

Reliance on a "generic favoritism or influence theory . . . is at odds with standard First Amendment analyses because it is unbounded and susceptible to no limiting principle."

The appearance of influence or access, furthermore, will not cause the electorate to lose faith in our democracy. By definition, an independent expenditure is political speech presented to the electorate that is not coordinated with a candidate. The fact that a corporation, or any other speaker, is willing to spend money to try to persuade voters presupposes that the people have the ultimate influence over elected officials. This is inconsistent with any suggestion that the electorate will refuse "'to take part in democratic governance'" because of additional political speech made by a corporation or any other speaker.

- *Do you agree with the logic of the Court's argument in the previous paragraphs? Does the electorate have nothing to fear from those who attempt to persuade voters by the use of large sums of money?*

... An outright ban on corporate political speech during the critical preelection period is not a permissible remedy. Here Congress has created categorical bans on speech that are asymmetrical to preventing quid pro quo corruption.

3   The government contends further that corporate independent expenditures can be limited because of its interest in protecting dissenting shareholders from being compelled to fund corporate political speech. This asserted interest, like *Austin's* antidistortion rationale, would allow the government to ban the political speech even of media corporations. Assume, for example, that a shareholder of a corporation that owns a newspaper disagrees with the political views the newspaper expresses. Under the government's view, that potential disagreement could give the government the authority to restrict the media corporation's political speech. The First Amendment does not allow that power. There is, furthermore, little evidence of abuse that cannot be corrected by shareholders "through the procedures of corporate democracy."

- *What does the Court believe a shareholder in a corporation could do if he or she disagreed with the political speech made by the corporation?*

Those reasons are sufficient to reject this shareholder-protection interest; and, moreover, the statute is both underinclusive and overinclusive. As to the first, if Congress had been seeking to protect dissenting shareholders, it would not have banned corporate speech in only certain media within 30 or 60 days before an election. A dissenting shareholder's interests would be implicated by speech in any media at any time. As to the second, the statute is overinclusive because it covers all corporations, including nonprofit corporations and for-profit corporations with only single shareholders. As to other corporations, the remedy is not to restrict speech but to consider and explore other regulatory mechanisms. The regulatory mechanism here, based on speech, contravenes the First Amendment.

- *What other reason does the Court give for not agreeing with the shareholder argument by the government?*

4   We need not reach the question whether the Government has a compelling interest in preventing foreign individuals or associations from influencing our Nation's political process. Section 441b is not limited to corporations or associations that were created in foreign countries or funded predom-

inately by foreign shareholders. Section 441b therefore would be overbroad even if we assumed, arguendo, that the Government has a compelling interest in limiting foreign influence over our political process.

- *The Court does not address the idea that the government has an interest in preventing influence by foreign individuals in the political process. Why might this issue come before the Court again, particularly after the election of 2016?*

C

Our precedent is to be respected unless the most convincing of reasons demonstrates that adherence to it puts us on a course that is sure error. "Beyond workability, the relevant factors in deciding whether to adhere to the principle of stare decisis include the antiquity of the precedent, the reliance interests at stake, and of course whether the decision was well reasoned."

These considerations counsel in favor of rejecting *Austin*, which itself contravened this Court's earlier precedents in *Buckley* and *Bellotti*. "This Court has not hesitated to overrule decisions offensive to the First Amendment."

- *What reason does the Court give for not following the precedent set by Austin?*

For the reasons above, it must be concluded that *Austin* was not well reasoned. *Austin* is undermined by experience since its announcement. Political speech is so ingrained in our culture that speakers find ways to circumvent campaign finance laws. Our Nation's speech dynamic is changing, and informative voices should not have to circumvent onerous restrictions to exercise their First Amendment rights. Speakers have become adept at presenting citizens with sound bites, talking points, and scripted messages that dominate the 24-hour news cycle. Corporations, like individuals, do not have monolithic views. On certain topics corporations may possess valuable expertise, leaving them the best equipped to point out errors or fallacies in speech of all sorts, including the speech of candidates and elected officials.

- *Do you agree that corporations may be the best equipped to point out errors in political ideas?*

Rapid changes in technology—and the creative dynamic inherent in the concept of free expression—counsel against upholding a law that restricts political speech in certain media or by certain speakers. Soon, however, it may be that Internet sources, such as blogs and social networking web sites, will provide citizens with significant information about political candidates and issues. Yet, §441b would seem to ban a blog post expressly advocating the election or defeat of a candidate if that blog were created with corporate funds. The First Amendment does not permit Congress to make these categorical distinctions based on the corporate identity of the speaker and the content of the political speech.

No serious reliance interests are at stake. Here, though, parties have been prevented from acting—corporations have been banned from making independent expenditures. Legislatures may have enacted bans on corporate expenditures believing that those bans were constitutional. This is not a compelling interest for stare decisis. If it were, legislative acts could prevent us from overruling our own precedents, thereby interfering with our duty "to say what the law is."

Due consideration leads to this conclusion: *Austin*, should be and now is overruled. We return to the principle established in Buckley and Bellotti that the Government may not suppress political speech on the basis of the speaker's corporate identity. No sufficient governmental interest justifies limits on the political speech of nonprofit or for-profit corporations.

D

Austin is overruled, so it provides no basis for allowing the Government to limit corporate independent expenditures. As the Government appears to concede, overruling Austin "effectively invalidate[s] not only BCRA Section 203, but also 2 U.S.C. 441b's prohibition on the use of corporate treasury funds for express advocacy." Brief for Appellee 33, n. 12. Section 441b's restrictions on corporate independent expenditures are therefore invalid and cannot be applied to *Hillary*.

Given our conclusion we are further required to overrule the part of *McConnell* that upheld BCRA §203's extension of §441b's restrictions on corporate independent expenditures. The McConnell Court relied on the antidistortion interest recognized in *Austin* to uphold a greater restriction on speech than the restriction upheld in *Austin*, and we have found this interest unconvincing and insufficient. This part of *McConnell* is now overruled.

IV

A

Citizens United next challenges BCRA's disclaimer and disclosure provisions as applied to *Hillary* and the three advertisements for the movie. Under BCRA §311, televised electioneering communications funded by anyone other than a candidate must include a disclaimer that "'_____ is responsible for the content of this advertising.'"

For the reasons stated below, we find the statute valid as applied to the ads for the movie and to the movie itself.

B

Citizens United sought to broadcast one 30-second and two 10-second ads to promote *Hillary*. Under FEC regulations, a communication that "[p]roposes a commercial transaction" was not subject to 2 U.S.C. §441b's restrictions on corporate or union funding of electioneering communications. The regulations, however, do not exempt those communications from the disclaimer and disclosure requirements in BCRA §§201 and 311.

Citizens United argues that the disclaimer requirements in §311 are unconstitutional as applied to its ads. It contends that the governmental interest in providing information to the electorate does not justify requiring disclaimers for any commercial advertisements, including the ones at issue here. We disagree. The ads fall within BCRA's definition of an "electioneering communication": They referred to then-Senator Clinton by name shortly before a primary and contained pejorative references to her candidacy.

Citizens United argues that §311 is underinclusive because it requires disclaimers for broadcast advertisements but not for print or Internet advertising. It asserts that §311 decreases both the quantity and effectiveness of the group's speech by forcing it to devote four seconds of each advertisement to the spoken disclaimer. We rejected these arguments in *McConnell*. And we now adhere to that decision as it pertains to the disclosure provisions.

As a final point, Citizens United claims that, in any event, the disclosure requirements in §201 must be confined to speech that is the functional equivalent of express advocacy. The Court has explained that disclosure is a less restrictive alternative to more comprehensive regulations of speech. [W]e reject Citizens United's contention that the disclosure requirements must be limited to speech that is the functional equivalent of express advocacy.

Citizens United also disputes that an informational interest justifies the application of §201 to its ads, which only attempt to persuade viewers to see the film. Even if it disclosed the funding sources for the ads, Citizens United says, the information would not help viewers make informed choices in the political marketplace. This is similar to the argument rejected above with respect to disclaimers. Even if the ads only pertain to a commercial transaction, the public has an interest in knowing who is speaking about a candidate shortly before an election. Because the informational interest alone is sufficient to justify application of §201 to these ads, it is not necessary to consider the Government's other asserted interests.

Last, Citizens United argues that disclosure requirements can chill donations to an organization by exposing donors to retaliation. Some amici point to recent events in which donors to certain causes were blacklisted, threatened, or otherwise targeted for retaliation. The examples cited by amici are cause for concern. Citizens United, however, has offered no evidence that its members may face similar threats or reprisals. To the contrary, Citizens United has been disclosing its donors for years and has identified no instance of harassment or retaliation.

Shareholder objections raised through the procedures of corporate democracy, see *Bellotti*, supra, at 794, and n. 34, can be more effective today because modern technology makes disclosures rapid and informative. A campaign finance system that pairs corporate independent expenditures with effective disclosure has not existed before today. It must be noted, furthermore, that many of Congress' findings in passing BCRA were premised on a system without adequate disclosure. With the advent of the Internet, prompt disclosure of expenditures can provide shareholders and citizens with the information needed to hold corporations and elected officials accountable for their positions and supporters. Shareholders can determine whether their corporation's political speech advances the corporation's interest in making profits, and citizens can see whether elected officials are "'in the pocket' of so-called moneyed interests." The First Amendment protects political speech; and disclosure permits citizens and shareholders to react to the speech of corporate entities in a proper way. This transparency enables the electorate to make informed decisions and give proper weight to different speakers and messages.

- *Citizens United did not win in its attempt to have a disclaimer removed from its film and advertisements. What reasoning did Citizens United give for the request of the removal? How did the Court respond?*

C

For the same reasons we uphold the application of BCRA §§201 and 311 to the ads, we affirm their application to *Hillary*. We find no constitutional impediment to the application of BCRA's disclaimer and disclosure requirements to a movie broadcast via video-on-demand. And there has been no showing that, as applied in this case, these requirements would impose a chill on speech or expression.

V

When word concerning the plot of the movie *Mr. Smith Goes to Washington* reached the circles of Government, some officials sought, by persuasion, to discourage its distribution. Under *Austin*, though, officials could have done more than discourage its distribution—they could have banned the film. After all, it, like *Hillary*, was speech funded by a corporation that was critical of Members of Congress. *Mr. Smith Goes to Washington* may be fiction and caricature; but fiction and caricature can be a powerful force.

- *Should an intentionally political creation be considered in the same manner as a commercial film that may have a political message?*

Modern day movies, television comedies, or skits on Youtube.com might portray public officials or public policies in unflattering ways. Yet if a covered transmission during the blackout period creates the background for candidate endorsement or opposition, a felony occurs solely because a corporation, other than an exempt media corporation, has made the "purchase, payment, distribution, loan, advance, deposit, or gift of money or anything of value" in order to engage in political speech. Speech would be suppressed in the realm where its necessity is most evident: in the public dialogue preceding a real election. Governments are often hostile to speech, but under our law and our tradition it seems stranger than fiction for our government to make this political speech a crime. Yet this is the statute's purpose and design.

Some members of the public might consider *Hillary* to be insightful and instructive; some might find it to be neither high art nor a fair discussion on how to set the Nation's course; still others simply might suspend judgment on these points but decide to think more about issues and candidates. Those choices and assessments, however, are not for the government to make. "The First Amendment underwrites the freedom to experiment and to create in the realm of thought and speech. Citizens must be free to use new forms, and new forums, for the expression of ideas. The civic discourse belongs to the people, and the government may not prescribe the means used to conduct it."

- *What is the Court assuming about those who listen to political discourse? Is it true today that most Americans "experiment and create" in their political thoughts?*

The judgment of the District Court is reversed with respect to the constitutionality of 2 U. S. C. §441b's restrictions on corporate independent expenditures. The judgment is affirmed with respect to BCRA's disclaimer and disclosure requirements. The case is remanded for further proceedings consistent with this opinion.

It is so ordered.

Connecting, Arguing, and Analyzing the Case

1. *Citizens United* expanded the First Amendment to corporations, a right traditionally given to individuals. What other cases have been

decided by the Supreme Court giving corporations the same rights as individuals? Do you think corporations should have the same rights as individuals?
2. Since the *Citizens United* decision, the United States has seen a rise in the attempts of super PACs to influence political elections. Debate the pros and cons of political action committees and whether they help candidates avoid campaign finance laws.
3. Under what circumstances could Congress create a campaign finance law that would sustain a First Amendment challenge using *Citizens United* as precedent?
4. In his dissent, Justice Stevens wrote the *Citizens United* decision would "undermine the integrity of elected institutions across the Nation" and he chastised the majority for ignoring stare decisis in its early rulings.

   a. Using information from the 2016 presidential election, write an argument where you either agree with the holding from *Citizen United* or disagree and support Justice Stevens's dissent.
   b. How important do you think it is that the Supreme Court abide by its previous rulings? What do you think needs to happen in order for the Court to overturn its opinion in full or in part, as it did in *Citizens United*?

Chapter Fifteen
McDonald v. Chicago

The Second Amendment to the U.S Constitution states, "A well regulated Militia, being necessary to the security of a free State, the right of the people to keep and bear Arms, shall not be infringed." This amendment essentially protects the rights of citizens to keep own and keep personal weapons, in addition to allowing the government to maintain a military force. However, as handguns have become easier to manufacture, smaller in size, and more prevalent in society, debate has ensued about whether states have the right to restrict the sale or ownership of guns to private citizens.

The Second Amendment, it seems, can be read in two ways: first, in a manner that reserves the federal government as the sole source of the militia, leaving the rights of individual citizens in question or second, in a manner that allows private citizens as well as the government to own weapons as a means of self-protection. As crime rates in large cities, like that of the city of Chicago in 1982 in this case, rose in dramatic proportions, politicians and legislatures sought to limit the ability for anyone to access handguns in order to minimize crime and violent deaths.

The *McDonald* case explores the concept of "selective incorporation," or how the first ten amendments to the Constitution (the Bill of Rights) apply to the states. Up until the end of the Civil War and prior to the passage of the Fourteenth Amendment, some states attempted to infringe on individual rights protected in the U.S. Constitution because the U.S. Constitution only applied to the federal government. The Fourteenth Amendment resolved this and ensured, over time, that individual rights in the U.S. Constitution were applicable to both state and federal government actors. Through a series of judicial decisions, eventually all rights set forth in the first eight amendments were applied to state governments through selective incorporation.

The most recent U.S. case law present dealing with whether the Second Amendment applied only to the federal government or to states and local municipalities took place in *District of Columbia v. Heller* (2008), in which the U.S. Supreme Court deemed a ban on handguns within the District of Columbia (a federal district, not an independent state) unconstitutional. The Court did permit some restrictions on weapons (for example, it supported the prohibition of a felon owning a handgun or that guns could be prohibited from school grounds) but in general supported the rights of citizens to own weapons of common use, like handguns used to protect one's house or property. Because that ruling really only applied to Washington, D.C. (not individual states), *McDonald* progressed through the judicial system to land with a similar issue at the Supreme Court.

Legal Issue

Does the Second Amendment right to keep and bear arms preclude states and local governments from banning gun ownership by citizens?

Vocabulary

Selective incorporation: A type of legal decision making that allows the U.S. Supreme Court to determine whether a right is fundamental or so important to an individual's liberty that it cannot be infringed upon by the state or federal government. If so, it is "incorporated" and protected through the Due Process Clause of the Fourteenth Amendment. If the right is not considered fundamental, the right may only be protected by the U.S. Constitution but not a state constitution. The process of "selective incorporation" arose when the Fourteenth Amendment was passed after the Civil War, protecting many rights of individuals under state and federal law.
Due process: the right of an individual to receive fair treatment under the law
Fundamental: Of primary or central importance. In legal cases, generally used when discussing whether an individual's right is "fundamental" or so basic to the root of humanity that it cannot or should not be infringed upon by the government.
Municipality: a city or town
Stare decisis: a legal process in which a court considers previous decisions when making a new decision
Precedent: "earlier laws or decisions that provide some example or rule to guide them in the case they're actually deciding" (Merriam-Webster)

Parties in the Case

Petitioner: Otis McDonald and three other Chicago residents (Adam Orlov, Colleen Lawson, and David Lawson
Respondent: City of Chicago
Edited version of case in the original language with distractors removed.

MCDONALD V. CHICAGO, 561 U.S. 742 (2010)

Two years ago, in *District of Columbia v. Heller* (2008), we held that the Second Amendment protects the right to keep and bear arms for the purpose of self-defense, and we struck down a District of Columbia law that banned the possession of handguns in the home. The city of Chicago (City) and the village of Oak Park, a Chicago suburb, have laws that are similar to the District of Columbia's, but Chicago and Oak Park argue that their laws are constitutional because the Second Amendment has no application to the States. We have previously held that most of the provisions of the Bill of Rights apply with full force to both the Federal Government and the States. Applying the standard that is well established in our case law, we hold that the Second Amendment right is fully applicable to the States.

I

Otis McDonald, Adam Orlov, Colleen Lawson, and David Lawson (Chicago petitioners) are Chicago residents who would like to keep handguns in their homes for self-defense but are prohibited from doing so by Chicago's firearms laws. A City ordinance provides that "[n]o person shall . . . possess . . . any firearm unless such person is the holder of a valid registration certificate for such firearm." The Code then prohibits registration of most handguns, thus effectively banning handgun possession by almost all private citizens who reside in the City. Like Chicago, Oak Park makes it "unlawful for any person to possess . . . any firearm," a term that includes "pistols, revolvers, guns and small arms . . . commonly known as handguns."

- *Think about the process of becoming a new gun owner in Oak Park/ Chicago. The city codes allow you to own a handgun but prohibit the required registration of a handgun, essentially making it impossible to own a gun. Does this seem fair? Does the fact that the area had a high crime rate change your thoughts?*

Chicago enacted its handgun ban to protect its residents "from the loss of property and injury or death from firearms." The Chicago petitioners, however, argue that the handgun ban has left them vulnerable to criminals. Chicago

Police Department statistics, we are told, reveal that the City's handgun murder rate has actually increased since the ban was enacted and that Chicago residents now face one of the highest murder rates in the country and rates of other violent crimes that exceed the average in comparable cities.

- *Reread the Second Amendment. Does it seem to protect citizens from violence? What does the language actually protect citizens from?*

Several of the Chicago petitioners have been the targets of threats and violence. For instance, Otis McDonald, who is in his late seventies, lives in a high-crime neighborhood. He is a community activist involved with alternative policing strategies, and his efforts to improve his neighborhood have subjected him to violent threats from drug dealers. Colleen Lawson is a Chicago resident whose home has been targeted by burglars. "In Mrs. Lawson's judgment, possessing a handgun in Chicago would decrease her chances of suffering serious injury or death should she ever be threatened again in her home." McDonald, Lawson, and the other Chicago petitioners own handguns that they store outside of the city limits, but they would like to keep their handguns in their homes for protection.

After our decision in *Heller*, the Chicago petitioners and two groups filed suit against the City in the United States District Court for the Northern District of Illinois. They sought a declaration that the handgun ban and several related Chicago ordinances violate the Second and Fourteenth Amendments to the United States Constitution. Another action challenging the Oak Park law was filed in the same District Court by the National Rifle Association (NRA) and two Oak Park residents. In addition, the NRA and others filed a third action challenging the Chicago ordinances. All three cases were assigned to the same District Judge.

- *Remember,* Heller *prohibited restrictions on most weapons only within Washington, D.C.—the Chicago residents want the same decision here.*

The District Court rejected plaintiffs' (the Chicago residents) argument that the Chicago and Oak Park laws are unconstitutional. The court noted that the Seventh Circuit had "squarely upheld the constitutionality of a ban on handguns a quarter century ago," and that *Heller* had explicitly refrained from "opin[ing] on the subject of incorporation vel non of the Second Amendment." The court observed that a district judge has a "duty to follow established precedent in the Court of Appeals to which he or she is beholden, even though the logic of more recent caselaw may point in a different direction."

The Seventh Circuit affirmed, relying on three nineteenth-century cases—*United States v. Cruikshank, Presser v. Illinois,* and *Miller v. Texas,* that were decided in the wake of this Court's interpretation of the Privileges or Immunities Clause of the Fourteenth Amendment in the *Slaughter-House Cases*. The Seventh Circuit described the rationale of those cases as "defunct" and recognized that they did not consider the question whether the Fourteenth Amendment's Due Process Clause incorporates the Second Amendment right to keep and bear arms. Nevertheless, the Seventh Circuit observed that it was obligated to follow Supreme Court precedents that have "direct application," and it declined to predict how the Second Amendment would fare under this Court's modern "selective incorporation" approach.

We granted certiorari.

II

A

Petitioners argue that the Chicago and Oak Park laws violate the right to keep and bear arms for two reasons. Petitioners' primary submission is that this right is among the "privileges or immunities of citizens of the United States" and that the narrow interpretation of the Privileges or Immunities Clause adopted in the *Slaughter-House Cases* should now be rejected. As a secondary argument, petitioners contend that the Fourteenth Amendment's Due Process Clause "incorporates" the Second Amendment right.

- *The Chicago residents bring up two potential arguments to support their right to own guns. What are those? Are the arguments convincing?*

Chicago and Oak Park (municipal respondents) maintain that a right set out in the Bill of Rights applies to the States only if that right is an indispensable attribute of *any* "'civilized'" legal system. If it is possible to imagine a civilized country that does not recognize the right, the municipal respondents tell us, then that right is not protected by due process. And since there are civilized countries that ban or strictly regulate the private possession of handguns, the municipal respondents maintain that due process does not preclude such measures. In light of the parties' far-reaching arguments, we begin by recounting this Court's analysis over the years of the relationship between the provisions of the Bill of Rights and the States.

B

The Bill of Rights, including the Second Amendment, originally applied only to the Federal Government. In *Barron ex rel. Tiernan v. Mayor of Baltimore*, the Court explained that this question was "of great importance" but "not of much difficulty." In less than four pages, the Court firmly rejected the proposition that the first eight amendments operate as limitations on the States, holding that they apply only to the Federal Government.

The constitutional Amendments adopted in the aftermath of the Civil War fundamentally altered our country's federal system. The provision at issue in this case, §1 of the Fourteenth Amendment, provides, among other things, that a State may not abridge "the privileges or immunities of citizens of the United States" or deprive "any person of life, liberty, or property, without due process of law."

- *Think about the constitutional amendments adopted after the Civil War, in particular the Fourteenth Amendment. Did that amendment say anything about applying the first ten amendments (the Bill of Rights) to the states? Why does that distinction matter?*

Four years after the adoption of the Fourteenth Amendment, this Court was asked to interpret the Amendment's reference to "the privileges or immunities of citizens of the United States." The *Slaughter-House Cases* involved challenges to a Louisiana law permitting the creation of a state-sanctioned monopoly on the butchering of animals within the city of New Orleans. Justice Samuel Miller's opinion for the Court concluded that the Privileges or Immunities Clause protects only those rights "which owe their existence to the Federal government, its National character, its Constitution, or its laws." The Court held that other fundamental rights—rights that predated the creation of the Federal Government and that "the State governments were created to establish and secure"—were not protected by the Clause.

- *What is the "privileges and immunities" clause of the Fourteenth Amendment? What does it mean in application?*

In drawing a sharp distinction between the rights of federal and state citizenship, the Court relied on two principal arguments. First, the Court emphasized that the Fourteenth Amendment's Privileges or Immunities Clause spoke of "the privileges or immunities of *citizens of the United States*," and the Court contrasted this phrasing with the wording in the first sentence of the Fourteenth Amendment and in the Privileges and Immunities Clause of Article IV, both of which refer to *state* citizenship. Second, the Court stated that a contrary reading would "radically chang[e] the whole theory of the relations of the State and Federal governments to each other and of both these governments to the people," and the Court refused to conclude that such a change had been made "in the absence of language which expresses such a purpose too clearly to admit of doubt." Finding the phrase "privileges or immunities of citizens of the United States" lacking by this high standard, the Court reasoned that the phrase must mean something more limited.

Under the Court's narrow reading, the Privileges or Immunities Clause protects such things as the right "to come to the seat of government to assert any claim [a citizen] may have upon that government, to transact any business he may have with it, to seek its protection, to share its offices, to engage in administering its functions . . . [and to] become a citizen of any State of the Union by a *bonâ fide* residence therein, with the same rights as other citizens of that State."

Finding no constitutional protection against state intrusion of the kind envisioned by the Louisiana statute, the Court upheld the statute. Four Justices dissented. Justice Field, joined by Chief Justice Chase and Justices Swayne and Bradley, criticized the majority for reducing the Fourteenth Amendment's Privileges or Immunities Clause to "a vain and idle enactment, which accomplished nothing, and most unnecessarily excited Congress and the people on its passage." Justice Field opined that the Privileges or Immunities Clause protects rights that are "in their nature . . . fundamental," including the right of every man to pursue his profession without the imposition of unequal or discriminatory restrictions. Justice Bradley's dissent observed that "we are not bound to resort to implication . . . to find an authoritative declaration of some of the most important privileges and immunities of citizens of the United States. It is in the Constitution itself." Justice Bradley would have construed the Privileges or Immunities Clause to include those rights enumerated in the Constitution as well as some unenumerated rights. Justice Swayne described the majority's narrow reading of the Privileges or Immunities Clause as "turn[ing] . . . what was meant for bread into a stone."

Three years after the decision in the *Slaughter-House Cases*, the Court decided *Cruikshank*, the first of the three 19th-century cases on which the Seventh Circuit relied. In that case, the Court reviewed convictions stemming from the infamous Colfax Massacre in Louisiana on Easter Sunday 1873. Dozens of blacks, many unarmed, were slaughtered by a rival band of armed white men. Cruikshank himself allegedly marched unarmed African-American prisoners through the streets and then had them summarily executed. Ninety-seven men were indicted for participating in the massacre, but only nine went to trial. Six of the nine were acquitted of all charges; the remaining three were acquitted of murder but convicted for banding and conspiring together to deprive their victims of various constitutional rights, including the right to bear arms.

The Court reversed all of the convictions, including those relating to the deprivation of the victims' right to bear arms. The Court wrote that the right of bearing arms for a lawful purpose "is not a right granted by the Constitution" and is not "in any manner dependent upon that instrument for its existence." "The second amendment," the Court continued, "declares that it shall not be infringed; but this . . . means no more than that it shall not be infringed by Congress." "Our later decisions reaffirmed that the Second Amendment applies only to the Federal Government."

- *Up until the* McDonald *case, the Court is saying provisions in the Second Amendment only apply to actions committed by the federal government. Think about what occurred in* Cruikshank—*and the fact that the people who slaughtered a group of black men were essentially exonerated because the Second Amendment only applied to rules that "infringed" on Congress's right to bear arms. Was that the correct interpretation of the Second Amendment? Why or why not?*

C

As previously noted, the Seventh Circuit concluded that *Cruikshank, Presser*, and *Miller* doomed petitioners' claims at the Court of Appeals level. Petitioners argue, however, that we should overrule those decisions and hold that the right to keep and bear arms is one of the "privileges or immunities of citizens of the United States." In petitioners' view, the Privileges or Immunities Clause protects all of the rights set out in the Bill of Rights, as well as some others, but petitioners are unable to identify the Clause's full scope. Nor is there any consensus on that question among the scholars who agree that the *Slaughter-House Cases*' interpretation is flawed.

We see no need to reconsider that interpretation here. For many decades, the question of the rights protected by the Fourteenth Amendment against state infringement has been analyzed under the Due Process Clause of that Amendment and not under the Privileges or Immunities Clause. We therefore decline to disturb the *Slaughter-House* holding.

- *The Court brings in the Due Process Clause of the Fourteenth Amendment, which says no one shall be denied "life, liberty, or property without due process of law." States are not allowed to make any law that violates life, liberty, or property of any its citizens without fair procedures for doing so.*

At the same time, however, this Court's decisions in *Cruikshank, Presser*, and *Miller* do not preclude us from considering whether the Due Process Clause of the Fourteenth Amendment makes the Second Amendment right binding on the States. None of those cases "engage[d] in the sort of Fourteenth Amendment inquiry required by our later cases." As explained more fully below, *Cruikshank, Presser,* and *Miller* all preceded the era in which the Court began the process of "selective incorporation" under the Due Process Clause, and we have never previously addressed the question whether the right to keep and bear arms applies to the States under that theory.

Indeed, *Cruikshank* has not prevented us from holding that other rights that were at issue in that case are binding on the States through the Due Process Clause. In *Cruikshank*, the Court held that the general "right of the people peaceably to assemble for lawful purposes," which is protected by the First Amendment, applied only against the Federal Government and not against the States. Nonetheless, over sixty years later the Court held that the right of peaceful assembly was a "fundamental righ[t] . . . safeguarded by the due process clause of the Fourteenth Amendment." We follow the same path here and thus consider whether the right to keep and bear arms applies to the States under the Due Process Clause.

- *What are fundamental rights in the Constitution?*

D

1 In the late nineteenth century, the Court began to consider whether the Due Process Clause prohibits the States from infringing rights set out in the Bill of Rights. Five features of the approach taken during the ensuing era should be noted.

First, the Court viewed the due process question as entirely separate from the question whether a right was a privilege or immunity of national citizenship.

Second, the Court explained that the only rights protected against state infringement by the Due Process Clause were those rights "of such a nature that they are included in the conception of due process of law." While it was "possible that some of the personal rights safeguarded by the first eight Amendments against National action [might] also be safeguarded against state action," the Court stated, this was "not because those rights are enumerated in the first eight Amendments."

The Court used different formulations in describing the boundaries of due process. For example, in *Twining*, the Court referred to "immutable principles of justice which inhere in the very idea of free government which no member of the Union may disregard." In *Snyder v. Massachusetts*, the Court spoke of rights that are "so rooted in the traditions and conscience of our people as to be ranked as fundamental." And in *Palko*, the Court famously said that due process protects those rights that are "the very essence of a scheme of ordered liberty" and essential to "a fair and enlightened system of justice."

- *How does the Court determine if something is a fundamental right?*

Third, in some cases decided during this era the Court "can be seen as having asked, when inquiring into whether some particular procedural safeguard was required of a State, if a civilized system could be imagined that would not accord the particular protection." Thus, in holding that due process prohibits a State from taking private property without just compensation, the

Court described the right as "a principle of natural equity, recognized by all temperate and civilized governments, from a deep and universal sense of its justice." Similarly, the Court found that due process did not provide a right against compelled incrimination in part because this right "has no place in the jurisprudence of civilized and free countries outside the domain of the common law."

Fourth, the Court during this era was not hesitant to hold that a right set out in the Bill of Rights failed to meet the test for inclusion within the protection of the Due Process Clause. The Court found that some such rights qualified. (freedom of speech and press); (assistance of counsel in capital cases); (freedom of assembly); (free exercise of religion). But others did not. (grand jury indictment requirement); (privilege against self-incrimination).

Finally, even when a right set out in the Bill of Rights was held to fall within the conception of due process, the protection or remedies afforded against state infringement sometimes differed from the protection or remedies provided against abridgment by the Federal Government. To give one example, in *Betts* the Court held that, although the Sixth Amendment required the appointment of counsel in all federal criminal cases in which the defendant was unable to retain an attorney, the Due Process Clause required appointment of counsel in state criminal proceedings only where "want of counsel in [the] particular case . . . result[ed] in a conviction lacking in . . . fundamental fairness." Similarly, in *Wolf v. Colorado*, the Court held that the "core of the Fourth Amendment" was implicit in the concept of ordered liberty and thus "enforceable against the States through the Due Process Clause" but that the exclusionary rule, which applied in federal cases, did not apply to the States.

- *Summarize the five reasons the Court lays out to utilize the Due Process Clause of the Fourteenth Amendment to help decide the outcome of the current case.*

2 An alternative theory regarding the relationship between the Bill of Rights and §1 of the Fourteenth Amendment was championed by Justice Black. This theory held that §1 of the Fourteenth Amendment totally incorporated all of the provisions of the Bill of Rights. As Justice Black noted, the chief congressional proponents of the Fourteenth Amendment espoused the view that the Amendment made the Bill of Rights applicable to the States and, in so doing, overruled this Court's decision in *Barron*. Nonetheless, the Court never has embraced Justice Black's "total incorporation" theory.

3 While Justice Black's theory was never adopted, the Court eventually moved in that direction by initiating what has been called a process of "selective incorporation," *i.e.*, the Court began to hold that the Due Process Clause fully incorporates particular rights contained in the first eight Amendments.

- *What is "selective incorporation" and how does it apply to the U.S. Constitution?*

The decisions during this time abandoned three of the previously noted characteristics of the earlier period. The Court made it clear that the governing standard is not whether *any* "civilized system [can] be imagined that would not accord the particular protection." Instead, the Court inquired whether a particular Bill of Rights guarantee is fundamental to *our* scheme of ordered liberty and system of justice (referring to those "fundamental principles of liberty and justice which lie at the base of all *our* civil and political institutions").

- *Why is Court making a distinction between whether any civilized system would pass laws versus whether "our" civilized system would allow the same laws?*

The Court also shed any reluctance to hold that rights guaranteed by the Bill of Rights met the requirements for protection under the Due Process Clause. The Court eventually incorporated almost all of the provisions of the Bill of Rights. Only a handful of the Bill of Rights protections remain unincorporated.

Finally, the Court abandoned "the notion that the Fourteenth Amendment applies to the States only a watered-down, subjective version of the individual guarantees of the Bill of Rights," stating that it would be "incongruous" to apply different standards "depending on whether the claim was asserted in a state or federal court." Instead, the Court decisively held that incorporated Bill of Rights protections "are all to be enforced against the States under the Fourteenth Amendment according to the same standards that protect those personal rights against federal encroachment."

Employing this approach, the Court overruled earlier decisions in which it had held that particular Bill of Rights guarantees, or remedies did not apply to the States.

III

With this framework in mind, we now turn directly to the question whether the Second Amendment right to keep and bear arms is incorporated in the concept of due process. In answering that question, as just explained, we must decide whether the right to keep and bear arms is fundamental to *our* scheme of ordered liberty, or as we have said in a related context, whether this right is "deeply rooted in this Nation's history and tradition,"

- *What is the nation's "history and tradition" of gun or weapon ownership? How has that changed over time?*

A

Our decision in *Heller* points unmistakably to the answer. Self-defense is a basic right, recognized by many legal systems from ancient times to the present day and in *Heller*, we held that individual self-defense is "the *central component*" of the Second Amendment right. Explaining that "the need for defense of self, family, and property is most acute" in the home, we found that this right applies to handguns because they are "the most preferred firearm in the nation to 'keep' and use for protection of one's home and family," (noting that handguns are "overwhelmingly chosen by American society for [the] lawful purpose" of self-defense; "The American people have considered the handgun to be the quintessential self-defense weapon"). Thus, we concluded, citizens must be permitted "to use [handguns] for the core lawful purpose of self-defense."

Heller makes it clear that this right is "deeply rooted in this Nation's history and tradition." *Heller* explored the right's origins, noting that the 1689 English Bill of Rights explicitly protected a right to keep arms for self-defense, and that by 1765, Blackstone was able to assert that the right to keep and bear arms was "one of the fundamental rights of Englishmen."

Blackstone's assessment was shared by the American colonists. As we noted in *Heller*, King George III's attempt to disarm the colonists in the 1760's and 1770's "provoked polemical reactions by Americans invoking their rights as Englishmen to keep arms."

- *The need (or desire) to keep weapons in one's home goes back to the Revolutionary War. Why was this such a concern at that particular point in history?*

The right to keep and bear arms was considered no less fundamental by those who drafted and ratified the Bill of Rights. "During the 1788 ratification debates, the fear that the federal government would disarm the people in order to impose rule through a standing army or select militia was pervasive in Antifederalist rhetoric." Federalists responded, not by arguing that the right was insufficiently important to warrant protection but by contending that the right was adequately protected by the Constitution's assignment of only limited powers to the Federal Government. Thus, Antifederalists and Federalists alike agreed that the right to bear arms was fundamental to the newly formed system of government. But those who were fearful that the new Federal Government would infringe traditional rights such as the right to keep and bear arms insisted on the adoption of the Bill of Rights as a condition for ratification of the Constitution. This is surely powerful evidence that the right was regarded as fundamental in the sense relevant here.

This understanding persisted in the years immediately following the ratification of the Bill of Rights. In addition to the four States that had adopted Second Amendment analogues before ratification, nine more States adopted state constitutional provisions protecting an individual right to keep and bear arms between 1789 and 1820. Founding-era legal commentators confirmed the importance of the right to early Americans. St. George Tucker, for example, described the right to keep and bear arms as "the true palladium of liberty" and explained that prohibitions on the right would place liberty "on the brink of destruction."

- *Does gun (or weapon) ownership ensure safety or security? Why or why not?*

B

1 By the 1850s, the perceived threat that had prompted the inclusion of the Second Amendment in the Bill of Rights—the fear that the National Government would disarm the universal militia—had largely faded as a popular concern, but the right to keep and bear arms was highly valued for purposes of self-defense. Abolitionist authors wrote in support of the right. And when attempts were made to disarm "Free-Soilers" in "Bloody Kansas," Senator Charles Sumner, who later played a leading role in the adoption of the Fourteenth Amendment, proclaimed that "[n]ever was [the rifle] more needed in just self-defense than now in Kansas." Indeed, the 1856 Republican Party Platform protested that in Kansas the constitutional rights of the people had been "fraudulently and violently taken from them" and the "right of the people to keep and bear arms" had been "infringed."

After the Civil War, many of the over 180,000 African Americans who served in the Union Army returned to the States of the old Confederacy, where systematic efforts were made to disarm them and other blacks. The laws of some States formally prohibited African Americans from possessing firearms. For example, a Mississippi law provided that "no freedman, free negro or mulatto, not in the military service of the United States government, and not licensed so to do by the board of police of his or her county, shall keep or carry fire-arms of any kind, or any ammunition, dirk or bowie knife."

- *Note that even after the Civil War was over, African Americans who served on the Union side were prohibited from owning weapons. Why?*

Throughout the South, armed parties, often consisting of ex-Confederate soldiers serving in the state militias, forcibly took firearms from newly freed slaves. In the first session of the 39th Congress, Senator Wilson told his colleagues: "In Mississippi rebel State forces, men who were in the rebel armies, are traversing the State, visiting the freedmen, disarming them, perpetrating murders and outrages upon them; and the same things are done in other sections of the country." In one town, the "marshal [took] all arms from returned colored soldiers, and [was] very prompt in shooting the blacks whenever an opportunity occur[red]." As Senator Wilson put it during the debate on a failed proposal to disband Southern militias: "There is one unbroken chain of testimony from all people that are loyal to this country, that the greatest outrages are perpetrated by armed men who go up and down the country searching houses, disarming people, committing outrages of every kind and description."

Union Army commanders took steps to secure the right of all citizens to keep and bear arms, but the 39th Congress concluded that legislative action was necessary. Its efforts to safeguard the right to keep and bear arms demonstrate that the right was still recognized to be fundamental.

The most explicit evidence of Congress' aim appears in §14 of the Freedmen's Bureau Act of 1866, which provided that "the right . . . to have full and equal benefit of all laws and proceedings concerning personal liberty, personal security, and the acquisition, enjoyment, and disposition of estate, real and personal, *including the constitutional right to bear arms*, shall be secured to and enjoyed by all the citizens . . . without respect to race or color, or previous condition of slavery." Section 14 thus explicitly guaranteed that "all the citizens," black and white, would have "the constitutional right to bear arms."

Congress, however, ultimately deemed these legislative remedies insufficient. Southern resistance, presidential vetoes, and this Court's pre-Civil-War precedent persuaded Congress that a constitutional amendment was necessary to provide full protection for the rights of blacks. Today, it is generally accepted that the Fourteenth Amendment was understood to provide a constitutional basis for protecting the rights set out in the Civil Rights Act of 1866.

In debating the Fourteenth Amendment, the 39th Congress referred to the right to keep and bear arms as a fundamental right deserving of protection. Senator Samuel Pomeroy described three "indispensable" "safeguards of liberty under our form of Government." One of these, he said, was the right to keep and bear arms:

"Every man . . . should have the right to bear arms for the defense of himself and family and his homestead. And if the cabin door of the freedman is broken open and the intruder enters for purposes as vile as were known to slavery, then should a well-loaded musket be in the hand of the occupant to send the polluted wretch to another world, where his wretchedness will forever remain complete."

Even those who thought the Fourteenth Amendment unnecessary believed that blacks, as citizens, "have equal right to protection, and to keep and bear arms for self-defense."

Evidence from the period immediately following the ratification of the Fourteenth Amendment only confirms that the right to keep and bear arms was considered fundamental. In an 1868 speech addressing the disarmament of freedmen, Representative Stevens emphasized the necessity of the right: "Disarm a community and you rob them of the means of defending life. Take away their weapons of defense and you take away the inalienable right of defending liberty." "The fourteenth amendment, now so happily adopted, settles the whole question."

- *Representative Stevens seems to believe the Fourteenth Amendment encompassed the rights within the Second Amendment for all citizens. Do you agree with his rationale?*

The right to keep and bear arms was also widely protected by state constitutions at the time when the Fourteenth Amendment was ratified. In 1868, 22 of the 37 States in the Union had state constitutional provisions explicitly protecting the right to keep and bear arms. Quite a few of these state constitutional guarantees, moreover, explicitly protected the right to keep and bear arms as an individual right to self-defense What is more, state constitutions adopted during the Reconstruction era by former Confederate States included a right to keep and bear arms. A clear majority of the States in 1868, therefore, recognized the right to keep and bear arms as being among the foundational rights necessary to our system of Government.

In sum, it is clear that the Framers and ratifiers of the Fourteenth Amendment counted the right to keep and bear arms among those fundamental rights necessary to our system of ordered liberty.

2 Despite all this evidence, municipal respondents contend that Congress, in the years immediately following the Civil War, merely sought to outlaw "discriminatory measures taken against freedmen, which it addressed by adopting a non-discrimination principle" and that even an outright ban on the possession of firearms was regarded as acceptable, "so long as it was not done in a discriminatory manner." They argue that Members of Congress overwhelmingly viewed §1 of the Fourteenth Amendment "as an antidiscrimination rule," and they cite statements to the effect that the section would outlaw discriminatory measures. This argument is implausible.

- *This argument that Section 1 of the Fourteenth Amendment only applies to discriminatory measures is complicated. Read the examples in the next paragraph to determine if the true intent of Section 1 is met if it applies only to discriminatory laws.*

First, while §1 of the Fourteenth Amendment contains "an antidiscrimination rule," namely, the Equal Protection Clause, municipal respondents can hardly mean that §1 does no more than prohibit discrimination. If that were so, then the First Amendment, as applied to the States, would not prohibit nondiscriminatory abridgments of the rights to freedom of speech or freedom of religion; the Fourth Amendment, as applied to the States, would not prohibit all unreasonable searches and seizures but only discriminatory searches and seizures—and so on. We assume that this is not municipal respondents' view, so what they must mean is that the Second Amendment should be singled out for special—and specially unfavorable—treatment. We reject that suggestion.

Second, municipal respondents' argument ignores the clear terms of the Freedmen's Bureau Act of 1866, which acknowledged the existence of the right to bear arms. If that law had used language such as "the equal benefit of laws concerning the bearing of arms," it would be possible to interpret it as simply a prohibition of racial discrimination. But §14 speaks of and protects "the constitutional right to bear arms," an unmistakable reference to the right protected by the Second Amendment. And it protects the "full and equal benefit" of this right in the States. 14 Stat. 176–177. It would have been nonsensical for Congress to guarantee the full and equal benefit of a constitutional right that does not exist.

Third, if the 39th Congress had outlawed only those laws that discriminate on the basis of race or previous condition of servitude, African Americans in the South would likely have remained vulnerable to attack by many of their worst abusers: the state militia and state peace officers. In the years immediately following the Civil War, a law banning the possession of guns by all private citizens would have been nondiscriminatory only in the formal sense. Any such law—like the Chicago and Oak Park ordinances challenged here—presumably would have permitted the possession of guns by those acting under the authority of the State and would thus have left firearms in the hands of the militia and local peace officers. And as the Report of the Joint Committee on Reconstruction revealed, those groups were widely involved in harassing blacks in the South.

Fourth, municipal respondents' purely antidiscrimination theory of the Fourteenth Amendment disregards the plight of whites in the South who opposed the Black Codes. If the 39th Congress and the ratifying public had simply prohibited racial discrimination with respect to the bearing of arms, opponents of the Black Codes would have been left without the means of self-defense—as had abolitionists in Kansas in the 1850s.

Fifth, the 39th Congress' response to proposals to disband and disarm the Southern militias is instructive. Despite recognizing and deploring the abuses of these militias, the 39th Congress balked at a proposal to disarm them. Disarmament, it was argued, would violate the members' right to bear arms, and it was ultimately decided to disband the militias but not to disarm their members. It cannot be doubted that the right to bear arms was regarded as a substantive guarantee, not a prohibition that could be ignored so long as the States legislated in an evenhanded manner.

- *The arguments set forth by the city seem to rely on the nation's prior history of needing to maintain order, protect slavery, and ensure state authority. How did the Court reject those arguments?*

IV

Municipal respondents' remaining arguments are at war with our central holding in *Heller*: that the Second Amendment protects a personal right to keep and bear arms for lawful purposes, most notably for self-defense within the home. Municipal respondents, in effect, ask us to treat the right recognized in *Heller* as a second-class right, subject to an entirely different body of rules than the other Bill of Rights guarantees that we have held to be incorporated into the Due Process Clause.

Municipal respondents' main argument is nothing less than a plea to disregard 50 years of incorporation precedent and return (presumably for this case only) to a bygone era. Municipal respondents submit that the Due Process Clause protects only those rights "recognized by all temperate and civilized governments, from a deep and universal sense of [their] justice." According to municipal respondents, if it is possible to imagine *any* civilized legal system that does not recognize a particular right, then the Due Process Clause does not make that right binding on the States. Therefore, the municipal respondents continue, because such countries as England, Canada, Australia, Japan, Denmark, Finland, Luxembourg, and New Zealand either ban or severely limit handgun ownership, it must follow that no right to possess such weapons is protected by the Fourteenth Amendment.

- *The Court provides examples of other "civilized" countries but notes that even if those countries do ban weapons ownership, the countries are also not subject to a unique set of democratic principles, like those of the U.S. Constitution. Does this make those other countries less civilized? Why or why not?*

This line of argument is, of course, inconsistent with the long-established standard we apply in incorporation cases. And the present-day implications of municipal respondents' argument are stunning. For example, many of the rights that our Bill of Rights provides for persons accused of criminal offenses are virtually unique to this country. If *our* understanding of the right to a jury trial, the right against self-incrimination, and the right to counsel were necessary attributes of *any* civilized country, it would follow that the United States is the only civilized Nation in the world.

Municipal respondents attempt to salvage their position by suggesting that their argument applies only to substantive as opposed to procedural rights. But even in this trimmed form, municipal respondents' argument flies in the face of more than a half-century of precedent. For example, in *Everson v. Board of Ed. of Ewing*, the Court held that the Fourteenth Amendment incorporates the Establishment Clause of the First Amendment. Yet several of the countries that municipal respondents recognize as civilized have established state churches. If we were to adopt municipal respondents' theory, all of this Court's Establishment Clause precedents involving actions taken by state and local governments would go by the boards.

Municipal respondents maintain that the Second Amendment differs from all of the other provisions of the Bill of Rights because it concerns the right to possess a deadly implement and thus has implications for public safety. And they note that there is intense disagreement on the question whether the private possession of guns in the home increases or decreases gun deaths and injuries.

The right to keep and bear arms, however, is not the only constitutional right that has controversial public safety implications. All of the constitutional provisions that impose restrictions on law enforcement and on the prosecution of crimes fall into the same category. Municipal respondents cite no case in which we have refrained from holding that a provision of the Bill of Rights is binding on the States on the ground that the right at issue has disputed public safety implications.

- *What other constitutional provisions relate to public safety?*

We likewise reject municipal respondents' argument that we should depart from our established incorporation methodology on the ground that making the Second Amendment binding on the States and their subdivisions is inconsistent with principles of federalism and will stifle experimentation. Municipal respondents point out—quite correctly—that conditions and problems differ from locality to locality and that citizens in different jurisdictions have divergent views on the issue of gun control. Municipal respondents therefore urge us to allow state and local governments to enact any gun control law that they deem to be reasonable, including a complete ban on the possession of handguns in the home for self-defense.

There is nothing new in the argument that, in order to respect federalism and allow useful state experimentation, a federal constitutional right should not be fully binding on the States. This argument was made repeatedly and eloquently by Members of this Court who rejected the concept of incorporation and urged retention of the two-track approach to incorporation.

McDonald v. Chicago 183

Throughout the era of "selective incorporation," Justice Harlan in particular, invoking the values of federalism and state experimentation, fought a determined rearguard action to preserve the two-track approach.

Time and again, however, those pleas failed. Unless we turn back the clock or adopt a special incorporation test applicable only to the Second Amendment, municipal respondents' argument must be rejected. Under our precedents, if a Bill of Rights guarantee is fundamental from an American perspective that guarantee is fully binding on the States and thus *limits* (but by no means eliminates) their ability to devise solutions to social problems that suit local needs and values. As noted by the 38 States that have appeared in this case as *amici* supporting petitioners, "[s]tate and local experimentation with reasonable firearms regulations will continue under the Second Amendment."

- *The Court does not limit all restrictions on gun ownership but says that the solutions must meet local needs and values* and *comply with the constitutional requirements. What would this type of law look like?*

Municipal respondents and their *amici* (supporters) complain that incorporation of the Second Amendment right will lead to extensive and costly litigation, but this argument applies with even greater force to constitutional rights and remedies that have already been held to be binding on the States. Consider the exclusionary rule. Although the exclusionary rule "is not an individual right," but a "judicially created rule," this Court made the rule applicable to the States. The exclusionary rule is said to result in "tens of thousands of contested suppression motions each year."

- *The exclusionary rule basically requires a court to exclude any evidence collected in an unconstitutional manner against an accused person. While this is not specifically forbidden by the Constitution, the Court has created this rule that essentially applies when interpreting the amendment in practice. How is this similar to the gun laws in this case?*

Municipal respondents assert that, although most state constitutions protect firearms rights, state courts have held that these rights are subject to "interest-balancing" and have sustained a variety of restrictions. In *Heller*, however, we expressly rejected the argument that the scope of the Second Amendment right should be determined by judicial interest balancing, and this Court decades ago abandoned "the notion that the Fourteenth Amendment applies to the States only a watered-down, subjective version of the individual guarantees of the Bill of Rights."

As evidence that the Fourteenth Amendment has not historically been understood to restrict the authority of the States to regulate firearms, municipal respondents and supporting *amici* cite a variety of state and local firearms laws that courts have upheld. But what is most striking about their research is the paucity of precedent sustaining bans comparable to those at issue here and in *Heller*. Municipal respondents cite precisely one case (from the late twentieth century) in which such a ban was sustained. It is important to keep in mind that *Heller*, while striking down a law that prohibited the possession of handguns in the home, recognized that the right to keep and bear arms is not "a right to keep and carry any weapon whatsoever in any manner whatsoever and for whatever purpose." We made it clear in *Heller* that our holding did not cast doubt on such longstanding regulatory measures as "prohibitions on the possession of firearms by felons and the mentally ill," "laws forbidding the carrying of firearms in sensitive places such as schools and government buildings, or laws imposing conditions and qualifications on the commercial sale of arms." We repeat those assurances here. Despite municipal respondents' doomsday proclamations, incorporation does not imperil every law regulating firearms.

- Does Heller *allow a person to own any weapon? Why or why not?*

Municipal respondents argue, finally, that the right to keep and bear arms is unique among the rights set out in the first eight Amendments "because the reason for codifying the Second Amendment (to protect the militia) differs from the purpose (primarily, to use firearms to engage in self-defense) that is claimed to make the right implicit in the concept of ordered liberty." Municipal respondents suggest that the Second Amendment right differs from the rights heretofore incorporated because the latter were "valued for [their] own sake." But we have never previously suggested that incorporation of a right turns on whether it has intrinsic as opposed to instrumental value, and quite a few of the rights previously held to be incorporated—for example the right to counsel and the right to confront and subpoena witnesses—are clearly instrumental by any measure. Moreover, this contention repackages one of the chief arguments that we rejected in *Heller*, i.e., that the scope of the Second Amendment right is defined by the immediate threat that led to the inclusion of that right in the Bill of Rights. In *Heller*, we recognized that the codification of this right was prompted by fear that the Federal Government would disarm and thus disable the militias, but we rejected the suggestion that the right was valued only as a means of preserving the militias. On the contrary, we stressed that the right was also valued because the possession of firearms was thought to be essential for self-defense. As we put it, self-defense was "the *central component* of the right itself."

V

A

We turn, finally, to the two dissenting opinions. Justice Stevens' eloquent opinion covers ground already addressed, and therefore little need be added in response. Justice Stevens would "'ground the prohibitions against state action squarely on due process, without intermediate reliance on any of the first eight Amendments.'" The question presented in this case, in his view, "is whether the particular right asserted by petitioners applies to the States because of the Fourteenth Amendment itself, standing on its own bottom." He would hold that "[t]he rights protected against state infringement by the Fourteenth Amendment's Due Process Clause need not be identical in shape or scope to the rights protected against Federal Government infringement by the various provisions of the Bill of Rights."

As we have explained, the Court, for the past half-century, has moved away from the two-track approach. If we were now to accept Justice Stevens' theory across the board, decades of decisions would be undermined. We assume that this is not what is proposed. What is urged instead, it appears, is that this theory be revived solely for the individual right that *Heller* recognized, over vigorous dissents.

The relationship between the Bill of Rights' guarantees and the States must be governed by a single, neutral principle. It is far too late to exhume what Justice Brennan, writing for the Court 46 years ago, derided as "the notion that the Fourteenth Amendment applies to the States only a watered-down, subjective version of the individual guarantees of the Bill of Rights."

B

Justice Breyer's dissent makes several points to which we briefly respond. To begin, while there is certainly room for disagreement about *Heller*'s analysis of the history of the right to keep and bear arms, nothing written since *Heller* persuades us to reopen the question there decided. Few other questions of original meaning have been as thoroughly explored.

Justice Breyer's conclusion that the Fourteenth Amendment does not incorporate the right to keep and bear arms appears to rest primarily on four factors: First, "there is no popular consensus" that the right is fundamental, second, the right does not protect minorities or persons neglected by those holding political power, third, incorporation of the Second Amendment right would "amount to a significant incursion on a traditional and important area of state concern, altering the constitutional relationship between the States and the Federal Government" and preventing local variations, and fourth, determining the scope of the Second Amendment right in cases involving state and local laws will force judges to answer difficult empirical questions regarding matters that are outside their area of expertise. Even if we believed that these factors were relevant to the incorporation inquiry, none of these factors undermines the case for incorporation of the right to keep and bear arms for self-defense.

- *Justice Breyer's dissent relies on several concepts, most notably that it might limit local laws that might be needed in specific areas of the country but not in others. Why would this be a problem?*

First, we have never held that a provision of the Bill of Rights applies to the States only if there is a "popular consensus" that the right is fundamental, and we see no basis for such a rule. But in this case, as it turns out, there is evidence of such a consensus. An *amicus* brief submitted by 58 Members of the Senate and 251 Members of the House of Representatives urges us to hold that the right to keep and bear arms is fundamental. Another brief submitted by 38 States takes the same position.

Second, petitioners and many others who live in high-crime areas dispute the proposition that the Second Amendment right does not protect minorities and those lacking political clout. The plight of Chicagoans living in high-crime areas was recently highlighted when two Illinois legislators representing Chicago districts called on the Governor to deploy the Illinois National Guard to patrol the City's streets. The legislators noted that the number of Chicago homicide victims during the current year equaled the number of American soldiers killed during that same period in Afghanistan and Iraq and that 80 percent of the Chicago victims were black. Supporting incorporation of the right to keep and bear arms contend that the right is especially important for women and members of other groups that may be especially vulnerable to violent crime. If, as petitioners believe, their safety and the safety of other law-abiding members of the community would be enhanced by the possession of handguns in the home for self-defense, then the Second Amendment right protects the rights of minorities and other residents of high-crime areas whose needs are not being met by elected public officials.

Third, Justice Breyer is correct that incorporation of the Second Amendment right will to some extent limit the legislative freedom of the States, but this is always true when a Bill of Rights provision is incorporated. Incorporation always restricts experimentation and local variations, but that has not stopped the Court from incorporating virtually every other provision of the Bill of Rights. "[T]he enshrinement of constitutional rights necessarily takes certain policy choices off the table." This conclusion is no more remarkable with respect to the Second Amendment than it is with respect to all the other limitations on state power found in the Constitution.

Finally, Justice Breyer is incorrect that incorporation will require judges to assess the costs and benefits of firearms restrictions and thus to make difficult empirical judgments in an area in which they lack expertise. As we have noted, while his opinion in *Heller* recommended an interest-balancing test, the Court specifically rejected that suggestion. "The very enumeration of the right takes out of the hands of government—even the Third Branch of Government—the power to decide on a case-by-case basis whether the right is *really worth* insisting upon."

In *Heller*, we held that the Second Amendment protects the right to possess a handgun in the home for the purpose of self-defense. Unless considerations of *stare decisis* counsel otherwise, a provision of the Bill of Rights that protects a right that is fundamental from an American perspective applies equally to the Federal Government and the States. We therefore hold that the Due Process Clause of the Fourteenth Amendment incorporates the Second Amendment right recognized in *Heller*. The judgment of the Court of Appeals is reversed, and the case is remanded for further proceedings.

It is so ordered.

Connecting, Arguing, and Analyzing the Case

1. How do we know if something is considered a "fundamental right"? Is there something you would consider a "fundamental right" that isn't included in the Bill of Rights? Why do you consider it to be fundamental and how would you convince a court of that? Create a comparison of what you consider to be your "rights" and identify why each should or should not be considered "fundamental."
2. The basic premise of the *McDonald* case is that rights listed in the U.S. Constitution should apply under both state and federal laws, not just at the federal level. Does this infringe on a state's ability to control its people unnecessarily? Why or why not?

    a. Consider the case of *Gideon v. Wainwright* where a man arrested and charged with felony breaking and entering requested a court-appointed attorney and was denied one under Florida state law. The U.S. Supreme Court overturned his conviction noting that the Sixth Amendment of the U.S. Constitution guarantees the right to be represented by counsel, even in state matters. How is this decision similar to the decision in *McDonald*?
    b. What gun regulations would stand under *McDonald*? Read how the mayor of Chicago responded to the pending *McDonald* decision in 2010, anticipating the city's laws would be struck down. The story can be found at: https://www.chicagotribune.com/news/ct-met-chicago-gun-ban-options-20100616-story.html.

3. Should individuals who are diagnosed with or have a history of mental disease be restricted from owning a gun? Consider a 2019 California law that enforces a lifetime ban on gun ownership for anyone involuntarily admitted into a mental health facility. Does this type of law follow the logic of *McDonald*? What about a gun law that requires a gun owner to meet a minimum age requirement, like 18 or 21?
4. In *Peruta v. San Diego County*, a lower court case in California, the city of San Diego sought to restrict concealed carry handguns by members of the general public by passing a strict law requiring someone wanting to own a handgun to provide "good cause" to do so. Debate ensued about whether a private citizen has the right to own a handgun and whether any citizen should be forced to show "good cause" to own a handgun under the Second Amendment. How does the San Diego law requiring additional documentation to own a handgun differ from that in the *McDonald* case? Is owning a handgun within the limits of the Second Amendment?

Index

abridging, 126
admonition, 110
adversary, 68
aggregate, 138
Amish, 102
amicus curiae, 58
anticorruption, 146
antidistortion, 146
apportionment, 44
assimilated, 102
averment, 30
axiom, 14

Baker v. Carr, 43, 44, 125, 134
Brown v. Board of Education of Topeka, 35, 36

censure, 102
checks and balances: in *Marbury v. Madison*, 11; in *New York Times Co. v. U.S.*, 89
Citizens United v. Federal Election Commission, 145, 146
civil liberty, 2
coercive, 58
cognizable, 44
colloquy, 68
commerce, 137
Commerce Clause: in *McCulloch v. Maryland*, 27; in *United States v Lopez*, 137, 139, 141, 142, 143

compelled, 76
compelling interest, 146
compulsory, 102
conscription, 30
constituency, 126

declaratory relief, 146
debasement, 44
diluted, 126
disparage, 30
doctrine, 58
due process, 166
Due Process Clause: in *Brown v. Board*, 40; in *Gideon v. Wainwright*, 69, 70, 71; in *McDonald v. Chicago*, 166, 169, 172, 173, 174, 175, 181, 185, 187; in *Roe v. Wade*, 113, 117, 120, 122

egregious, 126
enclaves, 76
Engel v. Vitale, 57, 58
enumeration, 44
Equal Protection Clause: in *Baker v. Carr*, 43, 50, 53, 54, 55; in *Brown v. Board*, 35; in *McDonald v. Chicago*, 180; in *Roe v. Wade*, 117, 122; in *Shaw v. Reno*, 125, 129, 130, 131, 132, 133
equity jurisdiction, 84
Establishment Clause: in *Engel v. Vitale*, 57, 59, 60, 61, 64; in *McDonald v. Chicago*, 182; in *Wisconsin v. Yoder*,

108
exigencies, 14
express advocacy, 146

Free Exercise Clause: in *Engel v. Vitale*,
60; in *Wisconsin v. Yoder*, 101, 102,
104, 105
freedom of the press: in *New York Times
Co. v. United States*, 83, 86, 87, 99
freedom of speech: in *Citizens United v.
FEC*, 149; in *Engel v. Vitale*, 57; in
McDonald v. Chicago, 180; in *New
York Times v. U.S.*, 83, 88; in *Schenck
v. United States*, 29, 30, 32; in *Tinker v.
Des Moines*, 75, 81
fundamental, 166

gerrymandering, 126
Gideon v. Wainwright, 67, 68, 187
Grandfather Cause, 126
Guaranty Clause: in *Baker v. Carr*, 50, 52,
53, 54

habeas corpus, 68

idiosyncrasies, 102
in forma pauperis, 68
injunction, 44, 84
injunctive relief, 146
intercourse, 138
interstate, 138
intrastate, 137
invoke, 58

judicial restraint, 84
jurisdiction, 2
justiciable, 44

layman, 68

mandamus, 2
Marbury v. Madison, 1, 2
McCulloch v. Maryland, 13, 14, 142
McDonald v. Chicago, 165, 167
municipality, 166

Necessary and Proper Clause: in
McCulloch v. Maryland, 13, 20, 21, 22,
27; in *United States v. Lopez*, 137

nascent, 76
necessary, 13
New York Times Co. v. United States, 83,
84
nondenominational, 58
nonjusticiability, 44
nugatory, 14

obstructive, 30

penumbras, 110
per curiam, 84
persecution, 58
precedent, 68, 166
predilection, 109
presumption, 84
pretextual, 126
procure, 110
prohibition, 76
prolixity, 14
propriety, 126
proscribing, 110
pseudonym, 110

quid pro quo, 146

rational basis, 138
reapportionment, 126
recitation, 58
regimentation, 76
right to counsel: in *Gideon v. Wainwright*,
67, 68, 71, 73; in *McDonald v.
Chicago*, 181, 184
Roe v. Wade, 109, 110

Schenck v. United States, 29, 30
Shaw v. Reno, 125, 126
substantive, 30
secular, 102
segregation, 35
selective incorporation, 166
separate but equal, 35
standing, 44
stare decisis, 146, 166
stigmatize, 126
strict scrutiny, 146
subject matter jurisdiction, 44

Tinker v. Des Moines Independent Community School District, 75, 76

uncouth, 126
undifferentiated, 76

United States v. Lopez, 137, 138

vintage, 110

Wisconsin v. Yoder, 101, 102

About the Authors

Gretchen Oltman, JD, PhD, has spent more than a decade in education as a high school teacher, university professor, and program administrator. Oltman earned a bachelor's of arts in English from the University of Nebraska–Lincoln, a master's of arts in teaching from the University of Louisville, a juris doctorate from the University of Nebraska College of Law, and a PhD in educational studies from the University of Nebraska. She is a licensed attorney in the state of Nebraska. Oltman currently serves as an assistant professor in the Interdisciplinary Studies Department at Creighton University in Omaha, Nebraska. Her first book, *Violence in Student Writing: A Guide for School Administrators*, was published in 2013. Her other coauthored books include *Law Meets Literature: A Novel Approach for the English Classroom*, *Prepare to Chair: Leading the Thesis and Dissertation Process*, and *The Themes that Bind Us: Simplifying Supreme Court Cases for the Social Studies Classroom*. She regularly presents at national conferences including those hosted by the National Council of Teachers of English, the AP Annual Conference, and the Education Law Association.

Johnna Graff, JD, earned a bachelor's of arts in English from Nebraska Wesleyan University and a juris doctorate with distinction from the University of Nebraska College of Law. She is a licensed attorney in the state of Nebraska. Graff is currently an English teacher at Lincoln Public School's Science Focus Program in Lincoln, Nebraska. Her teaching assignment includes Law and Literature. In addition, she is an adjunct instructor at Nebraska Wesleyan University and Doane University. She coauthored her first two books, *Law Meets Literature: A Novel Approach for the English Classroom* and *The Themes that Bind Us: Simplifying Supreme Court Cases for the Social Studies Classroom*, which were published by Rowman & Littlefield in

2015 and 2018. She presents at national conventions including the AP Annual Conference, the National Council of Teachers of English, the Conference on English Leadership, and the National Council for the Social Studies.

Cynthia Wood Maddux, JD, earned a bachelor's of arts in English from the University of Nebraska–Lincoln and a juris doctorate from the University of Nebraska College of Law. After spending nearly seven years as a practicing attorney and a nonprofit executive director, she received her postbaccalaureate teaching certification and began teaching high-school English in 2000. Along with Gretchen Oltman and Johnna Graff, Maddux coauthored her first book in 2015, *Law Meets Literature: A Novel Approach for the English Classroom*, published by Rowman & Littlefield. She is currently an English teacher at Lincoln North Star High School in Lincoln, Nebraska, and also serves as an adjunct instructor at Nebraska Wesleyan University. Maddux regularly presents at national conferences including the National Council of Teachers of English, the AP Annual Conference, and the Conference on English Leadership.

www.ingramcontent.com/pod-product-compliance
Lightning Source LLC
Chambersburg PA
CBHW022013300426
44117CB00005B/160